W9-BVJ-090

FEMINIST FAMILY THERAPY

The authors are the founders and faculty of
The Women's Institute for Life Studies, Houston, Texas

Cheryl Rampage and Barbara Ellman are joint second authors sharing
equal responsibility for this work.

Thelma Jean Goodrich, Ph.D., is Assistant Professor in the Department
of Family Medicine, Baylor College of Medicine, Houston, Texas.
Cheryl Rampage, Ph.D., is Associate Professor of Behavioral Sciences at
the University of Houston-Clear Lake, Houston, Texas.
Barbara Ellman, M.S.W., is Adjunct Professor at the University of
Houston Graduate School of Social Work, Houston, Texas.
Kris Halstead, M.S.Ed., is Associate Supervisor at the Family Therapy
Practice Center, Washington, DC.

A NORTON PROFESSIONAL BOOK

FEMINIST FAMILY THERAPY

A CASEBOOK

Thelma Jean Goodrich

Cheryl Rampage · Barbara Ellman

Kris Halstead

W. W. NORTON & COMPANY • NEW YORK • LONDON

The identifying characteristics of the individuals in this book such as name, occupation, etc., have been changed to protect the identity of our clients. In several cases, individuals are actually composite portraits.

Published simultaneously in Canada by Penguin Books Canada Ltd., 2801 John Street, Markham, Ontario L3R 1B4.

Printed in the United States of America.

First Edition

Library of Congress Cataloging-in-Publication Data

Feminist family therapy.

   1. Family psychotherapy. 2. Feminism.
I. Goodrich, Thelma Jean, 1940–
RC488.5.F45 1988   616.89'156   87-31297

ISBN 0-393-70050-X

W. W. Norton & Company, Inc., 500 Fifth Avenue, New York, N.Y. 10110
W. W. Norton & Company Ltd., 37 Great Russell Street, London WC1B 3NU

1 2 3 4 5 6 7 8 9 0

And often I have wondered
How the years and I survived
I had a mother who sang to me
An honest lullaby

— *Joan Baez, "Honest Lullaby"*

We dedicate this book to our mothers

Thelma Quillian Goodrich

Lois Mae Rampage   Frances Ellman

Mary Grzymkowski

whose love gave us the courage to question.

FOREWORD

Feminist Family Therapy is a casebook which presents a new way of conceptualizing and practicing family therapy. It represents a paradigm that acknowledges the gendered nature of the family and the intersection of gender with the family's material and psychic resources. I am impressed by the way the authors, Thelma Jean Goodrich, Cheryl Rampage, Barbara Ellman, and Kris Halstead, have devoted themselves to developing an approach that leaves behind the static models of sex role theory, functionalism, and stages in psychosexual development. By courageously acknowledging that the family exists in the context of a patriarchal society, they move beyond the ritual salutes often made by the field to the importance of the larger social context. Why "courageously"? Because in a society where we seek to obscure the inequities between men and women, we are made uncomfortable even by the use of the term, "patriarchy."

We sometimes forget that family therapy was born in a revolutionary movement, that of communications theory and systems challenges to linear models. Instead of the individually focused approach of psychoanalysis, family therapy offered a systemic view of relationships and concern for the context. But every revolution in time is destined to become conservative, to become "more of the same." The wizardry associated with pioneers like Gregory Bateson, Paul Watzlawick, and Virginia Satir has faded toward an establishment approach where we are concerned with refining and shaping its very circularity. Some see family therapy now as going around and around the same recursive loop.

In addition, our much admired and vaunted meta position has consistently turned a blind side toward gender, once more demonstrating how difficult it is to understand a system of which one is a part. As Judy Libow has pointed out, we have treated gender as a family secret. Thus, traditional family therapy has failed to enlighten families about the connection of their problems with culture-wide gender stereotypes and power relations. I believe family therapy is taking a giant step in now beginning to expose that secret, as this volume, Marianne Ault-Riche's, and others to come make apparent.

How can one achieve a paradigmatic shift? Feminist family therapists provide a challenge to the family therapy field, declaring that the revolution is not over. But, like all revolutions, this is resisted, even by old revolutionaries. Some theorists and practitioners will not be ready for these new ways of thinking about and working with families, labeling the call for change as political. But all social organization is politics, just as all meaning is semantics; every position involves "taking a standpoint." The question is not whether the standpoint is right or wrong, an unanswerable question in a postmodernist society, but what are the consequences of a particular standpoint. The standpoint of feminist family therapists leads to a model where women's complaints are not trivialized, women are not blamed for the family's problems, and women are not encouraged to stay in unhealthy and dangerous marriages.

As the authors remind us, family therapy is a moral endeavor, one based on a vision of human life, and the moral questions should not be obscured. Family therapy is transformative as well as adaptive to social norms. The authors point out how the problem of women's subordination in society has been marginalized, misunderstood, and ignored in family therapy. They unpack the male/female dichotomy. They move on from evaluation and critique to praxis. I admire their willingness to expose their own purposes and doubts in their case examples. They present an exquisite sensibility to their own attitudes, values, and responses to cultural norms and expectations. In honestly laying out the pitfalls as well as the advantages of their therapeutic approach, they have set a new standard for evaluating family therapy practice that other therapists might well emulate.

The meta position taken by this book is one that presents news of a difference. What difference is more pervasive than gender? Yet, difference does not have to mean deficit, as in psychoanalytic theories of women, or domination, as in structural and strategic theories where boundaries protect hierarchies. The therapy described in this book cuts across other approaches and truly places the family and the individual in the social context in a way previous approaches have seldom achieved.

The authors have worked as a team, developing, supporting, and critiquing one another in achieving this new approach. They have grounded their work in the ideas and articles on feminist family therapy that began to appear in the late 1970s. Their cases demonstrate how problems can be reframed to incorporate gender. In the case of a corporate marriage they show how depersonalized work structures impinge on the family. In another case they examine the stereotypes about single-parent families. The shibboleth of complementarity is exposed in another case where they point out that being one-down and taking a one-down position are not the same. Further cases focus on the family of origin and caretaking demands, a lesbian couple, and an abusive relationship. Through the case examples, the authors most tellingly reveal how gender role stereotypes constrict the desires, behavior, and development of all family members. They take tired terms, like fusion, boundary, and triangle, which have been drained of meaning, and give new meaning to them. They also revalorize dependency and endurance as equivalent to heroism and honor. And in drawing attention to women's position, they remind us that our systems theories cannot account for all phenomena: "whether the knife falls on the melon or the melon falls on the knife, it is the melon that gets hurt."

Can the revolution in family therapy continue? I suspect only with the infusion of a truly new conception, as is offered by feminist family therapy. The authors mention they are all the eldest in their families of origin. Who would not wish for such an eldest sister to show us the way? This book will be useful to many, many family therapists ready for a new paradigm. In *Feminist Family Therapy*, we share an enlarged and transformed vision of family therapy of the future.

Rachel T. Hare-Mustin
November 1987

CONTENTS

PREFACE

Only women hearing each other can
create a counterworld to the
prevailing sense of reality.

— *Mary Daly,*
Beyond God the Father

WE ARE FOUR family therapists who have each struggled in her own way to understand our work and our clients as we live in this patriarchal society. We are four women who have recognized in our own lives the insidious effects of sexism and the oppression that results from theories that degrade us. We found each other as friends and colleagues because we have been on the same journey — a journey toward understanding what we are doing and how we are surviving. We found each other through our declaration of ourselves as feminists. We found each other through a recognition of the failure of our respective training programs to prepare us to respond to the complexities of the American family and its individual members, particularly the women.

With great relief, we joined together, sharing office space and ideas, writing papers, making presentations, analyzing our work from our feminist perspective. In time, we established a forum for women to explore the feminist concerns and issues we all own. We called this forum The Women's Institute for Life Studies. Through workshops, seminars, retreats, consulting groups, salons, and celebrations, we created a space for women to become conscious, to have their consciousness raised.

It was not until we accepted the challenge given us by Susan Barrows of W. W. Norton that we understood the ramifications of all that shapes women's work. Our decision to write a book was much like a decision to have a baby together. This book is a part of all of us and our being in labor together stimulates our instincts to protect, name, feed, own, perfect, and make into our own image and likeness.

When we decided to write this book together, we made a commitment to develop a process which was collegial, respectful, and consensual. We decided not to divide up the book and each write a section, but rather to struggle together to produce theory born of our collective analysis. We met weekly to examine our beliefs about clients with whom we were currently working. Our goal was to respect each other's contribution and each other's way of making sense of therapeutic dilemmas, while maintaining ownership of our own. This was not always easy.

We are women, mothers, sisters, daughters, lovers, and mentors. We hail from the East Coast, the Midwest, and the Southwest; from Catholicism, Judaism, and Protestantism. We have all been married, some have divorced, some have lived in community. We all have daughters; two of us have sons. We are all the eldest in our family of origin. We all have a strong love for and devotion to women. All of this affects our work together. None of us is a woman of color and this affects our work together. None of us calls herself a lesbian and this affects our work together. While we were writing this book, one of us lost her father, one lost her mother, one birthed a baby, one adopted a baby, one moved away. These events affected our work together. The intertwining of our professional lives and our personal realities—and our knowing about that and using that—makes this project, our book, inherently feminist.

Along with women across the country, we are just beginning to learn what it is for women to work together, to create together, to cooperate and compete, confront and nurture. Too long have we all been deprived of such experience.

ACKNOWLEDGMENTS

MANY PEOPLE encouraged and supported our efforts in writing this book. We wish to thank them.

The works of Jean Baker Miller, Dorothy Dinnerstein, and Rachel Hare-Mustin stimulated our early thinking about the interface of feminism and family therapy. The members of the The Women's Project in Family Therapy—Betty Carter, Peggy Papp, Olga Silverstein and Marianne Walters—were pioneers in bringing gender issues to bear on family therapy. They have been generous in their enthusiasm for our work.

We also thank Susan Barrows, our editor at Norton. Susan's conviction that we were ready to write this book provided our initial inspiration, and her continued enthusiasm cheered us on when our energy flagged.

Our colleagues Lisa Balick and Linda Walsh demonstrated unceasing patience and good humor throughout months of distraction as we labored to finish the project. Their thoughtful reading of the manuscript resulted in numerous valuable suggestions.

Carol Snyder read several of the more troublesome chapters; her skill with the written word added clarity when obscurity threatened.

Margaret Nobles, our typist, was capable of transforming piles of dog-eared pages, scribbled on in four different illegible handwritings, into clean copies of intelligible prose. Her cheerfulness and astonishing efficiency were an enormous blessing as we struggled to meet deadlines.

Finally, we thank our clients—the ones whose stories are depicted here and the many others over the years who have challenged us to reshape our thinking about the process of therapy.

—T. J. G., C. R., B. E., K. H.

Acknowledgments from others have been my strength and stay: from Marianne Walters who affirmed my work at an early presentation and continued at subsequent presentations to encourage me in her special and personal way; from Betty Carter who both in print and in public forum let me know I was on target; from Lisa Balick and Loyce Baker who gave me daily assurance that there was a point to all my suffering; and from my children, my wonderful children—Dolly, Davey, Kelly, and Mila—who with all good grace stood aside for the extra work the last two years.

—T. J. G.

I thank my husband, Larry LaBoda, for assuming from the start that this work was important. His complete confidence that it would turn out well and his willingness to take up the slack at home provided enormous support. My children, Scott and Elizabeth, were patient in my absence and forgiving upon my return. The distraction they occasionally caused is insignificant compared to the joy they have always brought me.

—C. R.

I wish to thank my husband, Mitchell Aboulafia, who supported me with intellectual challenge, friendship, love, and extra parenting duty while I was wedded to the book. To Lauren, who blossomed into the neatest five year old overnight and was my wonderful treat when I came out of the cave. To Sara, who competed with the book in pregnancy and labor but has the clear distinction of emerging as the total joy she is. To my sister Susan and father Abe, who never tired of asking about "the book." To my friends, especially Hilary Karp and Susan Thal, who understood missed appointments, canceled dates, and unreturned phone calls. And finally to my neighbors, Nancy George and Sue Kellogg, who acted as extended family helping my family when I was unavailable.

—B. E.

Two people have given of their insights and time to critiquing parts of the manuscript. Caroline Whitbeck and Laurie Leitch have contributed in important ways to my understanding of the integration of feminist theory and practice. I acknowledge my gratitude to Lauro Halstead for his commitment to share with me his wisdom about the art of living and creating.

—K. H.

FEMINIST
FAMILY
THERAPY

I
FEMINISM AND THE FAMILY

> *This revolution is the most universal,*
> *most humane, and most human*
> *revolution of all. Who can be*
> *opposed to a revolution that asks,*
> *"How do we live with others? How*
> *do we bring up our kids? How is*
> *family life and work shared? How*
> *can we all be human?"*
>
> — *Jessie Bernard,* Women and the
> Public Interest

IN ITS MISSION to transform the very nature of the social order, feminism begins at home. The family takes a central place in feminist thinking for several reasons. First, the family serves as a fundamental source for the transmission of the norms and values of the culture — a culture under indictment by feminists at its very foundation. Second, the family is traditionally viewed as the domain of women and therefore deserves scrutiny by those concerned with the condition of women. Third, it is in the family that individuals first learn what it means to be male or female — definitions of self which feminists regard as highly problematic in our society.

When we speak of feminism, we speak of the philosophy which recognizes that men and women have different experiences of self, of other, of life, and that men's experience has been widely articulated while women's has been ignored or misrepresented. When we speak of feminism, we speak of the philosophy which recognizes that this society does not permit equality to women; on the contrary, it is structured so as to oppress women and uplift men. This structure is called patriarchy. When we speak of feminism, we speak of a philosophy which recognizes that every aspect of public and private life carries the mark of patriarchal thinking and practice and is therefore a necessary focus for re-vision.

Feminist analyses of the family start with placing the family in time, for definitions about valid membership and participation in family have varied over the ages according to political, economic, social, and individual need (Mintz and Kellogg, 1987; Morgan, 1966; Rabb and Rotberg, 1973). This perspective challenges the common belief that the family exists outside history, transcends history. It is erroneously assumed, for example, that "childhood" as a socially recognized developmental period has always existed. In fact, the emergence of childhood as we know it is connected to the development of the "modern family" during the era of the Industrial Revolution and thus is linked to changes in family structure, social class, economics, and demography which also occurred at that time (Aries, 1960/1962). This fact that even so seemingly fundamental a condition as childhood is actually a concept that is context-bound and ever-changing has entered neither the lay nor the professional consciousness. The origins of other features of family life are similarly disregarded, thus making those features seem to be natural — and constant — givens.

Consider the sharp division between the home (the domain of women) and the workplace (the world of men). It was industrialization with its capitalist economy that bifurcated Western society into two separate spheres supported by an ideology making one private and assigned to women, and the other public and assigned to men. Pre-industrialization had seen men and women working together even though there was some division of labor.

During the period of industrialization, a woman was systematically taught to become a preeminent housewife and mother over all other possible identities (for example: worker, lover, friend). Propaganda about the family entered into the family's home from every quarter, for a cadre of experts was created to educate, advise, and induct women into their new roles. Physicians, ministers, and the newly invented home economists took it upon themselves to prescribe to wives proper ways of behaving. These self-appointed experts created a host of manuals and other sets of instructions about child care and home care for women to consume.

Love itself was called upon as a way to galvanize women's attitudes and behaviors in the service of their exclusive role as housewife and mother. In fact, the term "housewife" was not created until industrialization. Similarly, although mothers have always existed, Motherhood as an institution had not (Rich, 1976). Women were taught, by the printed page and the pulpit, that they would be doing great harm to their husbands (who were in the world providing) and to their children (who, for the first time in history, were seen as needing special care) if they did not follow the advice and warnings of the experts.

Because of the compartmentalization of life produced by industrialization, women's role as keeper of the hearth came to be seen as essential to the culture. Wives were to make men's new positions as manufacturers and bureaucrats tolerable by creating and maintaining a nurturing and revitalizing home environment. The family was promoted as a private "haven" to compensate for the public "heartlessness" of the factories. A man's home had to appear to be his castle and he had to feel his new privilege of playing king to compensate for the alienation he now experienced in the workplace.

What of the women? Had the family become a haven, a safe and nurturing place for them? Feminists have written on the unsatisfying and vulnerable position of the housewife, beginning as far back as the 1890s when Charlotte Perkins Gilman wrote *The Yellow Wallpaper* (1973b). Gilman's story describes a wife's emotional decline as she hallucinates images on the wallpaper in the room she is confined to within her sheltered home. Ibsen's *A Doll's House* is another example of the forced infantilization of a wife by her husband (1985). Both these wives are told by their paternalistic husbands that what is happening to them is "for their own good" despite their discomfort. Even more significantly, they are told that their very goodness and identity as women will be questioned if they do not happily and quietly submit to their assigned place.

Contemporary feminists also have attempted to clarify the strange stirrings of discontent, isolation, and degradation experienced by housewives, beginning with Betty Friedan's *The Feminine Mystique* published in 1963 where "the problem that has no name" was exposed for all to see (Ehrenreich and English, 1978; Oakley, 1974; Swerdow, 1978). Yet it is still commonly believed that housewives are in a good arrangement, that they are well taken care of and could have no legitimate complaints. When "the happy homemaker" is shown in movies and novels to be subject to depression, alcoholism, or drug abuse, the situation is portrayed as idiosyncratic and personal, never political.

The home has not been nurturing for women, and worse, it has not even been safe for them, nor for their children. One in four wives is beaten by her husband and cases of incest, 97% of which are perpetrated by men, are estimated at 400,000 per year (Kosof, 1985; Straus, Gelles, and Steinmetz, 1980). These appalling figures are regarded as well below the actual incidence, and other acts of violence in the home such as marital rape and child-beating are equally difficult to count. What *is* reported makes it impossible to hold the comforting thought that violent and abusive men are a fringe element. Our culture has not merely allowed men to believe that they have power over their wives and children; it has actively created and reinforced men's dominant position.

Feminists have exposed the relationship between violence — sexual, physical, and emotional — and the privacy of the home as a place for the exercise of male prerogative (Dobash and Dobash, 1979; Herman, 1982; Russell, 1982; Schecter, 1982). That ideology of privacy continues to silence thousands of victims of domestic violence. Adherents to the ideology call for a hands-off policy by the state and claim that involvement by government in family life is un-American. Feminists point out that this American government has been (and should be) involved in family life in many ways: compulsory education, mandatory immunization, regulations concerning housing, regulations concerning health and safety, control of information about and access to birth control and abortion, and child labor laws (Norgren, 1982). Most recently, the family-as-island stance has been undermined by laws that require institutional involvement with families where there is "reason to believe" neglect or abuse of children. An additional though late-incoming provision permits a wife to defend herself against her husband. The assumption that what goes on "behind closed doors" is not society's business must be overruled by a commitment to more fundamental individual or human rights. No husband has the right to beat his wife. No parents have the right to beat their children.

Questions about how women and children fare in the home are

only possible with a shift in perspective, for it has generally been assumed that what is good for the family (read: husband) is good for all (read: wife and children). Consider the contrast offered by de Beauvoir (1974): "We hold that the only public good is that which assures the private good of the citizens; we shall pass judgement on institutions according to their effectiveness in giving concrete opportunities to individuals" (p. xxxiii). It is this position we take here in judging the institution called the family. We evaluate all activities, attitudes, policies, and behaviors as they affect the individuals in the family, a process which means recognizing not only the husband/father/man but the wife/mother/woman and each child. Seeing them as individuals instead of a reified family forces an acknowledgement that the individuals in the family are not equal—not in status, resources, or power. Husband/father/man has more of each. As long as women and children are subordinate in a culture and in a family where men are dominant, women and children are in danger. To look to society for protection of its weaker members is asking the fox to guard the chickens, for despite recent reforms, society promotes both the weakness and the danger.

Gender Role Stereotypes and the Family

Sex is a biological category referring to maleness or femaleness. Gender is a social construct and entails the assignment of certain social tasks to one sex, others to the other sex. These assignments define what are labeled masculine or feminine and represent social beliefs about what it means to be male and female in a given society at a particular period in time. Gender stereotyping results from regarding designated behaviors, attitudes, and feelings as appropriate to only one sex. All of us act as if these are real, i.e., natural differences, rather than socially shaped; we forget that sex refers only to anatomical difference.[1]

Gender roles have been organized in a manner that places men

[1]In her book, *Feminism Unmodified,* Catharine A. MacKinnon (1987) asserts that men, the dominant gender, assumed the power to define both difference and the difference gender makes. Since our understandings of sexual difference are masculine constructions, though typically presented as objective theories and discoveries, she concludes that the biological and the social are inseparable in this area. For our purposes, however, we will continue to use the term sex to mean biological category and gender to mean social category.

in a dominant position, women in a subordinate one (Miller, 1976). This arrangement underlies all surface distinctions between men and women and produces most task assignments. Those tasks that the dominants choose for themselves become the tasks of high worth and status; those they confer on the subordinates are seen as having low worth and status. Subordinates do not typically get to choose, unless the dominants allow the choice, which is really not choosing. This arrangement precludes the possibility of equality and reciprocity between the sexes, narrows the range of possible behaviors for both sexes, and leads to rigidity and polarization. Most importantly, it asserts and maintains men as powerful, women as powerless.

The family is a social unit that expresses society's values, expectations, roles, and stereotypes. It teaches the culture's approved gender roles by treating and responding to girls and boys differently, holding different expectations for them, and exerting different social pressures on them. By thus producing the familiar boy/man and girl/woman, the family performs a critical function for society.

Another way the family functions as the training ground for gender roles is by enacting those roles. Father as the "head" of the family supports the notion of "father" as head of the country, leader of the people, and recognized authority in the world. Mother as the "caretaker" of the family supports the stereotype of woman as nurturer, harmonizer, peacekeeper of the world.

The culture's methods of training children in their gender roles teach us from a young age *not* to see gender as a social construct, but rather to see it as deeply rooted in human nature. "Boys don't play with dolls," is meant to shame a boy into believing that he is not behaving properly as a male if he displays behavior supposedly suited to girls. This injunction holds the obvious implication of "going against nature." It hides the fact that the culture, not nature, determines what is appropriate behavior for each sex. We grow up blind to social learning and believe we are what we were meant to be as destined by our anatomical structure.

Underlying gender-based assignments are three central assumptions about male and female roles: (1) Men believe they should always have privilege and the right to control women's lives; (2) women believe they are responsible for whatever goes wrong in a human relationship, and (3) women believe men are essential for their well-being—essential rather than merely desirable or enjoyable. These three assumptions combine to create most of the interactions as well as the problems between men and women. The first two are obviously manifestations of the powerful individual (male) over the powerless individual (female), both individuals deriving their status solely by virtue of their gender. To experience oneself as male in this society is to experience privilege. To experience oneself as female in this society is to experience personal responsibility for relationships. The third assumption partially explains what keeps women connected to the powerful. Subordinates need to stay in the good graces of the dominants in order to exist. Although it is true that the master requires a slave in order to be a master as well as the slave requires a master in order to be a slave, the actual material existence and experience of each is far from identical. The feminist perspective elucidates not only the differences between the genders but the power of one over the other.

Gender role stereotyping hurts families. It constricts and limits the desires, expectations, behavior, and development of individuals in the family. In married couples, gender role stereotyping often results in partners resenting each other precisely because they fulfill their gender roles. For example, the wife becomes angry because her husband will not talk to her about his problems. What had appeared at a distance to be the strong, silent man becomes in daily interaction the insulated, withholding husband. Or, the husband becomes angry because his wife is always nagging him. What had appeared at a distance to be the tenaciously nurturing woman becomes in close focus the stubborn shrewish wife.

The Ideology of the "Normal" Family

Prevailing concepts of the "normal" family constitute an ideology based on gender role stereotypes: father as breadwinner and head of the household; mother as full-time homemaker, helpmate to husband, caretaker of all. As is true of all ideologies, this one creates a vision to work towards, a sociopolitical program of assertions, theories, and aims. As such, it holds enormous sway over the expectations and evaluations of both lay and professional observers of family. The fact that the "normal" family has declined sharply in number has had little effect on the dominion of the ideology, a dominion that feminists regard as harmful in a number of ways.

First, the role prescribed for the woman in the "normal" family is oppressive. Certainly, the role prescribed for the husband injures him, but the hurts are not equal. Although both husband and wife are deprived of experiencing aspects of themselves not permitted in the arrangement, the wife has additional burdens. The common division of labor excludes the wife from direct access to valued resources such as income, authority, and status-decreed work. Her unpaid labor (housework, raising the children, community volunteer work) is not valued. Even when the wife works outside the home, she still carries the burden of the vast majority of household and child care responsibilities, leaving her with a tenuous attachment to the work force and little upward mobility. Generally, the woman has given up more to be married than the man has (her occupation, friends, residence, family, name). She adjusts to his life. Studies show that whereas marriage adds to men's physical and mental well-being, it subtracts from women's. (See research reported in Bernard, 1982.)

Second, the ideology of the "normal" family is pernicious in its effects on other family forms. Homosexual couples, single parents, couples without children, communal arrangements — are all termed "alternative" even though they outnumber "normal" arrangements (Masnick and Bane, 1980). These "alternatives" are implicity labeled deviant. The poverty and isolation which often characterize these familes — falsely attributed to faulty structure — actually issue from the prejudice created by the narrow definition of "normal" and enacted in the workplace both economically and socially.

Feminists, then, are committed to countering the ideology of the "normal" family because of its inaccurate representation of actual families, its harmful prescription for women, its stigmatizing of other arrangements, in short, because it is based on a single notion of class (middle), race (white), religion (Protestant), affectional preference (heterosexual), and gender privilege (male). In its challenge and clarification, feminist study of the family instructs us to see families as they are, rather than as icons. Feminist study also instructs us to examine all arrangements for competence as well as damage, brilliance as well as perversity. For feminists, the aim is not to save any particular form of family but to ensure that the needs of every individual are well-served.

The Feminist Challenge

Feminists call for reconstruction of terms and development of models that can better illuminate the contradictions and consequences at the point of interaction between gender, power, family, and society. Contemporary terms and models rest on dualist constructions such as instrumental/expressive, rational/emotive, objective/subjective, mind/body. Feminists recognize that these constructs are essentially evaluative and actually function as a hierarchy in which one side is treated as superior to the other. The culturally determined descriptors "masculine/feminine," set up as opposing categories and attached to the biological categories male/female, are one more example of the dualistic hierarchy that pervades everyday life, thought, and language. Chapters IV, VI, and VII all demonstrate that polarization, ignorance, resentment, denigration, and imbalances of power are directly related to this gender duality.

Feminists point out the inherent bias within Western society that dictates which set of characteristics is superior to the other. Instrumental, rational, objective, and mind, are held in greater esteem than expressive, emotive, subjective, and body. It is not accidental that the superior set is associated with the male, the inferior with the female. This valuation appears most blatantly in the bureaucratic language of our times, dominated as it is by the idiom of technology. It is a language that reflects masculine values: the adherents of instrumentalism solve the problem of dualism by eliminating the expressive sphere altogether. Simultaneously abrupt and convoluted, drained of emotion, pretending objectivity, overwhelmingly mechanical, and without subject, this language relies on passive and impersonal construction, creating the effect that there are no actors, that no one is acting upon anything or anyone, that things are happening totally apart from human will (French, 1985). This obliteration of the personal occurs, for example, in the following hospital jargon, "therapeutic misadventure resulting in a terminal episode," instead of death by medical malpractice (Satchell, 1987).

Feminists challenge the claim that this language is objective and value-free, and further, challenge the claim that having no values — that is, no explicit morality — is desirable. Confusion results so that we violate our own knowing in order to be consistent with what we have come to believe is "unbiased" thinking. The battle over Baby M is a case in point. The genetic, childbearing mother was called "surrogate mother" because the process — hiring via a contract — was judged to be a more essential reality than the biological reality itself (Safire, 1987). The mystifying objectivity of official language is designed to conceal inequities, violence, persons, passion, the "I and Thou," and it has come to pervade even those fields that are about human relationship, human encounter, and human feelings. For example, family therapists who use the term "spousal abuse" participate in concealing the predominant reality of the violent husband as perpetrator, wife as victim. Zealous to keep up with the language of technology, science, and business, many family therapists have even abandoned "family" for "cybernetics" and "individuals" for "consumers." (See Watzlawick, Weakland, and Fisch, 1974.)

Within feminism, there are several ideas about how to address dualism and its representation in language. Some feminists suggest making the opposite category the superior one, thereby inverting the hierarchy within dualistic thinking. They view expressivism as superior to instrumentalism, and all that is associated with being female as superior to that which is associated with being male. In this schema, the subjective has all-importance, with particular emphasis on female imagery, bodily references, and feelings. Experimentation with syntax, words, and punctuation reflects this fundamental re-ordering (e.g. Mary Daly, 1978; Susan Griffin, 1978).

Other feminists want to re-value and celebrate feminine qualities through language without claiming them superior. They assert that it would be in everyone's best interest (men as well as women, children, the planet) if the less valued side in the hierarchical relation were raised to a level of esteem matching the contrasting set (Miller, 1976; Dinnerstein, 1977). Revalorization is our intent in Chapter VII, in which dependency, which has been viewed by the culture as feminine and bad, is called human and good, and in

Chapter IX, where endurance is understood as the female equivalent to heroism and honor. We thereby take qualities judged as inferior, again not coincidentally associated with being female, and make them understood as good.

Revalorization of characteristically womanly traits will never be more than partial as long as human potentials are split off into assignments, some to women, some to men. Most assuredly and obviously is this the case if women remain subordinate to men. As a different solution, some feminists suggest synthesism, "a dialectical fusion of reason and emotion" (Glennon, 1983, p. 263). Dualistic thinking teaches us to choose between opposing categories, while a dialectic approach affords us a path of synthesis, of union. Chapter V demonstrates synthesism by focusing on single mothers in general and the black mother in particular as models of an expressive/instrumental union.

Finally, feminists call for the construction of new meanings, directed towards allowing individual persons to become more intelligible to themselves (Elshtain, 1982). Chapter VIII is our attempt at such reconceiving. Fusion, boundary, triangle—terms that have been at the center of family therapy—are reworked by our staying close to the subjective experience of our clients.

We began this chapter noting that feminists take the family as a primary focus for examination and challenge. Indeed, the most provoking actions by feminists have been those that relate to family life: working to re-distribute household and mothering responsibilities, validating nontraditional sexual and living arrangements, stressing the importance of ending women's economic dependence on men, fighting for reproductive rights, rejecting men's authority and privilege. Involvement with family pushes feminists into close and highly charged encounter with other organized projects which focus on family, for example, with family therapy. In Chapter II, we encounter family therapy.

II
FEMINIST FAMILY THERAPY: TOWARD REFORMATION

. . . if we disregard the condition of
women, our family therapy may be
not worth doing. And, I submit,
therapy that is not worth doing, is
not worth doing well.

— *Rachel Hare-Mustin,*
Family Therapy of the Future:
A Feminist Critique

FEMINIST FAMILY THERAPY is the application of feminist theory and values to family therapy. More specifically, feminist family therapy examines how gender roles and stereotyping affect (1) each individual in the family, (2) relationships between individuals in the family, (3) relationships between the family and society, and (4) relationships between the family and the therapist. To make these effects explicit allows the family to consider a wider range of perspectives, behaviors, and solutions, a range less constricted by rigid definitions of role and identity, by rigid ways of defining, possessing, and exercising power. Traditional family therapy has done nothing to enlighten families about the connection of their own troubles to culture-wide gender stereotypes and power relations, and furthermore, has no theory that links the interactions of family members to the larger social system. Feminist theory offers such a linkage.

The goal is change, not adjustment; social change, family change, individual change, with intent to transform the social relations which define men's and women's existence. On the way, the reformation of family therapy is unavoidable. Two things must be said about reformation. First, reformation is marked by conflict within and without, as well as by passion, hope, and devotion. Second, the outcome produced by reforming an established body of doctrine and practice often bears less resemblance to the original than was envisioned at the outset.

So be it.

Our thesis is that family therapy has accepted prevailing *gender roles*, ignoring their oppression of women, and accepted a traditional *family model*, ignoring its oppression of women. This failure to notice has resulted in *theory*, *practice*, and *training* that are oppressive to women. The remainder of this chapter, and indeed of this book, discusses the major terms of our thesis.[1]

Gender roles. Family therapy has worked within the given of gender roles as traditionally constituted, without question, without criticism, without assessment of their impact. This consistent inattention to the actual content, process, and outcome of prescribed gender roles is curious in a field which takes the family as its centerpiece, curious since gender roles are key determinants of the structure and functioning of family life, curious also since the family is the place where gender roles are compellingly taught and presented. In addition, gender roles shape relationships in the family, creating the dilemmas which underlie most of what is heard about in therapy. Father-daughter, mother-son, mother-daughter, father-son twist into the tangles they do precisely because mother and father are enacting traditional gender roles and teaching daughter and son to do so as well. These gender roles have gone unchallenged in family therapy. It is ironic that a field that champions second-order change never took on this level of analysis.

Even with regard to that prototypical clinical family described as enmeshed mother, peripheral father, and generic children, where the same sex keeps playing the same part in family after family,

---

[1]Some of our discussion parallels discussions written by other feminist family therapists, who in turn are parallel at times. Rather than making repetitive citations, we list all pertinent references later in this chapter as resources for training.

family therapy has not raised key questions: What does it signify that this pattern is so ubiquitous? What built-in assumptions keep producing it? Should these assumptions be left alone or not? Raising such questions could expose the bias inherent in the formulation "enmeshed mother/peripheral father." As Walters points out, the description is "implicitly critical of the mother and self-serving for the father" (Walters, 1984, p. 25). Cultural expectations are that mother will be primary caretaker and father will be primary provider and therefore peripheral to daily family life except for being central as decision-maker and power-broker. Sincere enactment of these expectations often leads to serious problems. Family therapy's response has been to blame the players (mostly mother) rather than the script, not addressing the gender role prescriptions which form definitions of self that produce the trouble. Feminist family therapists are pursuing this task.

Family model. Family therapy's acceptance of traditional gender roles is accompanied by acceptance of the traditional model of family with its gendered division of labor. Fewer than 15% of American families today have the breadwinner/homemaker form (Masnick & Bane, 1980), but this version of family and its distribution of roles, rights, and responsibilities still prevails ideologically. Even when the mother works outside the home, she is regarded in family therapy as having primary responsibility for the children, and her career as well as her personal needs are treated as second in importance to her husband's. (Research supporting this statement is cited in Avis, in press.) The scandal in holding onto this version of family goes beyond its statistical marginality. The scandal is that family therapy has held onto this version despite its unfairness to women, and despite at least two decades of research and theory detailing the destructive and distorting effects of the arrangement it depicts. (Much of this research and theory is reviewed in Thorne, 1982.)

Regardless of whether wives work outside the home or not, it is still common for the husband to function as head of the household and to have the lion's share of the power. Distribution of power is neither a chance occurrence nor an interpersonal affair. It is a class affair and is structurally predetermined: the class of men is dominant over the subordinated class of women. Family therapists have generally disregarded this differential in power; some have even recommended working with the assumption that men and women have equal power until proven otherwise (Pittman, 1985). However, the proof that power distribution is unequal has never seemed to point toward a change in theory. Each incident is treated as a unique occurrence, or perhaps a natural occurrence, never adding up to the general oppression of women. Consider even economic power, where the differential of women to men is so dramatic. Most family therapists have not included this reality in their formulations, and have remained silent about its effects on interactions within the family.

As Goldner observes, "Women have always been buried in families. . . ." (1985a, p. 45). Women have also been buried in family therapy. The psychological, legal, and social obstacles put in the way of women's gaining equality—even in the family itself—have been absent from theory, practice, and training in this field.

Theory

If not purposeful, it is at least convenient that family therapy has had systems theory as its primary way of seeing and thinking, a theory both too abstract and too concrete to generate any challenge to patriarchal outlook. By "convenient," we mean that systems theory allows practitioners to work without disturbing their apparent commitment to not know about women's condition either in the family or in the world. Systems theory is so abstract that it provides a seemingly coherent account while actually leaving out critical variables. The critical variables we have in mind are gender and power. Since systems theory focuses entirely on the moves rather than the players, who has power over whom never has to be noticed.

Systems theory is also too concrete in that it maintains a narrow focus on each individual, particular family. Patterns across families reflecting large-scale oppression of women in society are thus kept from entering or troubling the field of vision and discourse. Scholarly work from other disciplines on women's condition and its connection to the conventional model of family is also excluded (e.g., Bernard, 1973; Rich, 1976; Thorne, 1982; Tilly and Scott, 1978). Family theorists and therapists blinded to these data have a distorted and distorting perspective.

Criticisms of systems theory notwithstanding, the condition of women in families—even one family at a time—should have been obvious. Why it was not obvious—or if obvious, not commented on—is the subject of much speculation by feminists. It ought to be the subject of much soul-searching by family therapists, for we are describing here not merely an academic failure, but a moral failure. It is a moral failure because theorists and practitioners have produced and continue to defend theory and practice that allow oppression to be left out of everyone's awareness—the therapists', the oppressors', and worst of all, the victims'.

The consequences are extensive. As Hare-Mustin has noted, "When we alter the internal functioning of families without concern for the social, economic, and political context, we are in complicity with the society to keep the family unchanged" (1987, p. 20). Additionally, when we concern ourselves with the internal functioning of families without altering the power differences, we are in complicity with the society to keep women oppressed.

Let us examine some specific constructs prompting this indictment of systems theory. *Complementarity*, a systemic concept applied to an observed inequality between partners to an interaction is the first example. When applied to marital exchanges, complementarity easily glosses over the fact that it is wives who are regularly and ultimately at a disadvantage, living as they do in an arrangement that has been structured by law, social custom, and religious doctrine to ensure that positioning. This fact cannot find any entry point into the concept of complementarity.

Complementarity assumes that an observed inequality in an interaction is only temporary and play-acting. At a deeper level of reality, so it goes, the partners are actually equal; they began as equals, will be equal again, and, in fact, will likely switch places in the next unequal exchange. Consistent positioning by any particular player, if even noticed, is dismissed as having no harmful consequence because, it is argued, there is disguised power in helplessness and paradoxical strength in weakness. This is the sort of reframing useful for making the less powerful party feel fine about being so. Under complementarity, the reality of structured oppression is defined out of existence.[2]

Circularity is another systemic construct that operates in women's disfavor. The idea that people are involved in recursive patterns of behavior, reactively instigated and mutually reinforced, results either in making everyone equally responsible for everything or no one accountable for anything. This notion works differentially against women because a wife does not have the power and resources to be equal to her husband in influencing what happens in family life, yet she is held equally responsible, or no one is. This reasoning leaves her falsely blamed and him home free.

Does she nag because he drinks or does he drink because she nags? This familiar query passes for a deep philosophical conundrum, but for it to function as a puzzle requires a massive disregard for the woman's plight. One reading trivializes her complaint by putting it down to the same level as "pick up your socks." The other reading suggests that the consequences of nagging are every bit as bad as the consequences of drinking. Either way, she is no more or less involved, accountable, or hindered than he. We could describe the differences in the lopsided distribution of favorable options facing a husband and a wife in such a situation, but more to the point is the absurdity and harm exposed in circular descriptions once gender and power are considered.

"This woman has been beaten by her husband" is a good start towards a linear (i.e., "wrong") description of wife-battering, better known in the field, unfortunately, as spouse abuse or couple violence. "What had she done?" is the standard response. The outrage of the act and the violence of the actor are lost in theoretical discussions about punctuating an infinite regression of events. That gambit also dismisses the suffering. As the old proverb teaches: whether the knife falls on the melon or the melon falls on the knife, it is the melon that gets hurt. No matter how the first two clauses of the proverb are combined and the event redescribed, the outcome remains stubborn fact.

Neutrality, or multilateral partiality, is a stance recommended

---

[2]Later chapters in this book contain further discussion about complementarity. In Chapter VI, we offer an additional illustration of the potential for bias against women that is hidden in this apparently neutral construct. In Chapter VII, we show how using complementarity can mask a complex problem for both sexes related to gender role stereotyping.

by systems theorists for the therapist to hold so that each member of the family feels sided *with* and no one feels sided *against*. This stance obviously parallels the other systemic constructs discussed here that are aimed at holding either everyone or no one responsible. Every time the issues in therapy are distinctly sexist, the therapist perpetuates the inequality by being evenhanded.

For example, the therapist may try to keep suggested changes equal, or try to make the consequences of change equal. Two people in an unequal power relation who each give up in some way 10% of their power are still in the same power relation as before. Further, the consequences of shifts towards equality are not equally inviting. When the goal is equality, the husband will necessarily leave therapy feeling less privileged than when he arrived, and the wife will feel more privileged.

In situations of wife-beating and other abuse, the actual bias against women inherent in remaining neutral or being evenhanded has been explained. It is important to note that even in less dramatic situations, the therapist who takes a neutral position adds weight to the sexist side. Even silence from a person of authority such as a therapist can easily be understood as assent to the presented inequality, whether or not the family recognizes the arrangement as problematic.

The intended blamelessness of circularity, complementarity, and neutrality which masks a bias against women when applied to wife-battering breaks down altogether when Mother can be a target. The most outrageous example is to blame her for her husband's sexual abuse of their children. Incest is blatant testimony to the old adage that power corrupts. By turning the light on Mother—her failure to satisfy her husband, her failure to enact a proper executive role, her failure to stand guard, her failure to know—a therapist conceals the reproaching truth that domination by Father can lead to abuse. Father's absolute power as head of the household can corrupt absolutely.

Not only incest, but many and varied ills of family life and individual behavior are blamed on Mother. This is a predictable outcome when psychological theory locates the formation of character in childhood, and family therapy supports the view that childhood is mother's work. Surveys of family therapy journals show our field to be pervaded by mother-blaming (Caplan and

Hall-McCorquodale, 1985). By looking toward Mother for blame, one ignores Father, the principle of power, and the morality of power. (See Chapter VI for further discussion.)

In addition to systems theory, there is also a problem in family therapy with regard to the descriptions and prescriptions of what constitutes adulthood and mature relationships. We refer to the concepts of fusion, enmeshment, individuation, differentiation, and boundaries, all of which focus on how essential it is for people to keep a healthy distance from other people and from the emotional parts of themselves. Male values permeate these formulations, depicting a stand-on-your-own-two-feet ethos which holds autonomy as the highest good, emotion and intimacy as dangers to it, and power over others as a sure sign of having attained it.

This masculine outlook is shaped by man's journey towards selfhood (Chodorow, 1978; Dinnerstein, 1976). Man only becomes himself and becomes aware of his identity as a masculine being by separating himself from his mother. He learns to know himself through renunciation: "I am the sum of characteristics of the not-female." The resulting emphasis on autonomy is not only accepted uncritically in family therapy as an ideal for men to continue, but is held out for women as well and thus becomes presented as the ideal for all human beings.

Because women's journey towards selfhood is so different from men's, using men's development and values as paradigmatic makes women look like failures. Women too are reared by Mother; however, they develop alongside someone like them, someone whose qualities they are encouraged to mimic and incorporate. As a result, women experience relationship as life-giving. A woman knows herself through an other with whom she is involved in mutual responsiveness. Autonomy and differentiation are included as aspects of connectedness, not as opposing forces. She comes to know herself by close engagement (Chodorow, 1978; Dinnerstein, 1976).

Women are right about this matter. There is no self without an other, and the challenge is to integrate autonomy and connection. One reason a man can look so enviably strong and separate is because women are playing out the other side for him. Mother, sister, daughter, wife, secretary, and lover are absorbed in his reality, doing the work of supporting, holding, and connecting as he courageously goes into the world, apparently alone. Women will only be able to present themselves as strong and separate in the way men do if they are supported in the way men are. Either women must provide such support to one another or wait until men are reared differently so that they will know how to provide it for us—and want to.

So much of the literature in family therapy is about getting separate and staying separate, and so little is about getting connected and staying connected. This emphasis suggests that by knowing how to separate, people can do the relatively simpler task of connecting, a skill less valued and, not surprisingly, associated with women. Family therapy has not challenged the dichotomy of the categories (autonomy versus connection), has not challenged the hierarchy (autonomy over connection), and has not challenged the outcome: the seemingly separate man viewed as superior to the reliably connecting woman.

Given the marked potential for harm that we have outlined, it is an urgent task that feminist family therapists have undertaken in reviewing, reforming, and rewriting theory. To date, the feminist critique of family therapy theory has been elaborated more fully than has the feminist proposal, but the work has well begun. We make our contribution to it throughout the chapters of this book. We want to avoid the mistake of not mentioning what matters. We therefore make plain in each clinical case the values that undergird the theoretical analysis guiding our therapy. We say that:

—Both men and women are accountable for the quality of marital and family life.

—Rather than rigid role definition and difference, good relationships are marked by mutuality, reciprocity, and interdependency.

—Clients who learn about the source and implication of their beliefs have keys to liberation.

—All people responsible for fostering the growth of our children are charged both with nurturing them and with helping them be proficient in the world outside the home.

—Family structure does not need to be hierarchical to carry out family functions, rather let it be democratic, responsive, consensual.

—The respect, love, and safety required for the best of human growth and enjoyment are equally possible in a variety of constellations: lesbian relationships, single-parent families, dual career couples, and others.

— Connection and autonomy are to be equally sought, and each is a necessary condition for the other.

— Power, as so far exercised by men, fathers, and husbands, is not to be more equally shared but banished altogether and replaced by giving one's skills and influence towards the well-being of others just as one also does for one's own well-being.

Practice

A still frequently encountered misconception about feminist family therapy presumes that it is a set of techniques used to rescue "good" women from being victimized by "bad" men. This presumption contains two essential errors. First, feminist family therapy is not a set of techniques, but a political and philosophical viewpoint which produces a therapeutic methodology by informing the questions the therapist asks and the understanding the therapist develops. Second, the approach has nothing to do with blaming and rescuing, for these techniques are simply indicative of bad therapy, and can never be excused on the basis of their supposed political correctness.

Developing the practice of feminist family therapy begins as therapists become aware of their own values regarding gender and examine the extent to which their ideas about the differences between men and women are based on sexist stereotypes. Ideas about family and about other ways of relating can then be newly evaluated. This process will lead therapists to reform both their theories and practice of therapy, rejecting some concepts outright, altering others, and creating new ones.

It is the responsibility of the therapist to address gender issues and make them explicit to the family precisely because the family cannot see its problems as gender related. We are all trained not to see gender as manufactured and thus have internalized stereotypes to such a degree that they feel like truths. Moreover, in the dominant/subordinate system in which men and women interact, neither side is supposed to comment on the arrangement. As a result, family members believe that their problems are idiosyncratic and their gender arrangements unremarkable. Because they confuse biological sex with socially prescribed gender roles, they assume that gender related behavior is natural, unavoidable, and immutable. This assumption excludes an enormous range of human behavior as a topic for analysis and change. For example, the common saying "boys will be boys" instructs the listener to take some piece of behavior as a given, not subject to further discussion, let alone alteration.

By making gender a topic, the feminist family therapist enlarges and transforms the context of the family's presented problems. The therapist asks questions that make explicit issues, decisions, and behaviors that demonstrate to what degree equality and reciprocity exist in the family. For example, discussing with a couple the reasons for the husband's comfort with his direct and voluble expression of anger and his wife's indirect expression of the same emotion can raise a host of issues about the rest of their gender arrangements.

Since the therapist is also gendered and gender is never neutral, the therapist's behavior will always either reinforce or challenge the family's assumptions about gender. Typically, the family begins interacting with the therapist on the basis of traditional stereotypes, thus female therapists and male therapists will face different problems. For example, a female therapist may find the family looking to her for rescue, and because of her gender role training, she may feel pulled to respond. A male therapist may find the husband chumming with him and the wife asking for advice. Because of his gender role training, he may feel pulled to cooperate. For therapists to deny the impact of gender on their relationships with families means missing not only a powerful dynamic but also the opportunity to use gender role in a therapeutic manner.

The feminist family therapist works quite consciously with the notion that use of self in therapy means use of a gendered self. A primary goal is to embody alternatives to the narrow definition of woman and man which the clients have likely brought to therapy. Ideally the family will see in the feminist family therapist a woman or man who combines skills usually taken to be mutually exclusive and belonging to one sex only. That is, the family will have a therapist who exercises authority, displays competence, and draws boundaries, and at the same time demonstrates empathy, respect, nurturance, and careful listening. This combination of skills is unusual and unexpected, and will therefore stand out in the clients' minds against their usual experience of human behavior which is defined by stereotypes.

The kind of relationship which the feminist family therapist wants to create with the clients is one in which the clients experience the therapist as honest, confrontive, expressive, challenging, safe, kind, trustworthy, benevolent, mannerly, understanding, attentive, patient, respectful, tolerant, consistent, relaxed, cooperative, unshockable, and unprejudiced. Further, the clients experience the therapist as committed to, though not necessarily in agreement with, each person involved. Such a relationship is a necessary but not sufficient condition for producing the changes the clients seek. It is the medium and the context of the therapy.

This therapeutic relationship becomes manifest in the therapy as the clients expose the ways they think about themselves in the world, and the therapist challenges that thinking on the basis of its accuracy, completeness, or usefulness. Without experiencing a trusting and respectful relationship, clients would not tolerate these challenges, however gently they were presented. Without the relationship, the therapist would not have the credibility with the clients to offer alternatives, to stop familiar patterns, and to suggest novel solutions.

At the level of problem analysis, feminism will inform the questions which the therapist considers regarding the family. The questions are not necessarily posed directly to the family but guide the therapist's observations:

(1) How are gender stereotypes affecting the allocation of labor, power, and rewards in this family?
(2) How do the stereotypes and the consequent allocations of labor, power, and rewards interact with the presenting problem?
(3) What do the family members believe about manly and womanly labor that makes labor be distributed the way it is and prevents its distribution some other way? (This question refers to parenting and nurturant functions, as well as household chores, financial control, and breadwinning.)

(4) What do family members believe about manly and womanly power that makes power be distributed the way it is and prevents its distribution some other way?

(5) What do family members believe about manly and womanly desires, worth, values, and entitlement that makes rewards be distributed the way they are and prevents their distribution some other way?

(6) What solutions have been closed off to the family because of their uncritical acceptance of sexist values?

(7) Given the answers to questions 1–6, what will the family be likely to expect from me, given my gender? Where shall I expect trouble between us? Where can I make the easiest dent in their customary expectations? Where will I feel the most vulnerable to their expectations?

(8) What other pressures, wishes, and relationships are involved in shaping their problem and their attempts at solution in addition to gender role stereotypes (understanding that all these other factors will be mediated by their gender role stereotypes)?

From the answers to these questions, the therapist forms an analysis of the meaning gender has for the clients. The therapist uses this analysis to guide interactions with the family in a way that challenges and frees them from their narrow definitions of maleness and femaleness, questioning the family's assumptions about who is responsible for childcare, decision making, housework, sexual frequency, breadwinning, and birth control. By interacting with the clients in ways that are empowering, validating, and demystifying, the therapist helps them generate alternative behaviors, values, and feelings. These changes may sometimes occur on a very large scale—a couple decides that the wife will go to work and the husband will stay home with the children—but more typically the changes involve a series of smaller shifts: she experiments with directly expressing her anger, he practices being aware of and naming his feelings. Such shifts take place not only because of what the clients observe about the therapist, but because of how they experience themselves when their typical role-prescribed attitudes and behaviors are blocked, reinterpreted, directly questioned, or rerouted by the therapist.

For example, when the therapist instructs an emotionally with-drawn father to express without words the way he feels about his son, the father is forced to expand his capacity to demonstrate affection or to confront whatever it is that prevents him from doing so. Such moves require the family to re-evaluate routine attitudes and behavior, intentionally invent new behavior, or discover that they have suddenly and spontaneously emitted unaccustomed behavior. Thus change is produced not simply because the thera-pist instructs it, but through the interaction with the therapist, the clients experience themselves differently. First they recognize an incongruence between customary expectation and what they now experience, then the therapist helps them integrate these be-haviors.

The feminist family therapist uses a variety of techniques drawn from various schools of family therapy, but will be sensitive not to use any technique that is sexist or oppressive. For example, refram-ing is a powerful therapeutic technique that a feminist family thera-pist would be just as likely to use as a non-feminist family thera-pist. A feminist family therapist, however, would never use reframing in the manner demonstrated by Bergman (1987) to sug-gest that the real problem with a male client who abuses alcohol and drugs is the presence of too many women in his family. Even if such a reframe could shift the system, a feminist family therapist would decry its use since it vindicates the abusive man and leaves the women feeling responsible and blamed. The fact that such interventions have been used suggests that therapists relate to women with the same ambivalence as does the rest of society, seeing them as the gatekeepers and nurturers of the family and resenting them for that power.

The therapist's sensitivity to gender will affect the shape, tim-ing, and other features of interventions. For example, a traditional family therapist and a feminist family therapist may both deem it desirable in a given situation to help the wife work through her ambivalence about taking a paid job outside the family. It is likely that both therapists will correctly estimate the difficulty this shift will represent for the husband. The feminist family therapist, how-ever, is more likely than the traditional family therapist to estimate correctly the great difficulty this shift will represent for the wife: her fear of breaching their marital contract, her regret at disloyalty coupled with fear of reprisal for threatening what has been her husband's prerogatives, and perhaps her fear of losing unquestioned claim to being a womanly woman. Recognizing the woman's concerns, the feminist family therapist will take steps that are framed and supported differently than those by the traditional family therapist.

For instance, the feminist family therapist will make the foregoing analysis explicit to the couple, discussing with them the threat the wife's changing may present to her husband, the retaliations she may face, and the guilt she may feel. Sharing the analysis validates the woman's experience, demystifies her about her reluctance to change, and empowers her to make an informed decision for herself by helping her get information and resources. For the husband, the therapist's predictions about his feeling threatened may paradoxically allow him to feel more prepared for and accepting of this change.

When a family comes to therapy, it is usually at the instigation of a mother/wife, because keeping the family functioning smoothly is seen by everyone in the family as *her* job. She enters therapy feeling that somehow whatever has gone wrong is her fault exclusively. In traditional therapy, she then encounters a therapist who spends a large part of the session talking to *her* rather than to other members of the family. This focus is not necessarily because the therapist shares the view that mother is responsible for the well-being of the family (although the therapist may do just that), but rather because the therapist finds it so much easier to talk to the woman who is trained in the language of feelings and notices subtle nuances of behavior. These skills and her sense of responsibility make mother highly motivated, and the therapist uses mother's motivation as leverage for change. The husband/father may be implicitly excused from meaningful participation in the therapy. His mere presence is accepted as sufficient. This differential attitude by the therapist reinforces the gender role stereotypes held by the clients, the therapist, and the culture at large. In contrast, the feminist family therapist will not accept ineptitude as an excuse for non-participation in therapy, and therefore will persist in asking questions and making assignments directed to both spouses which indicate that responsibility for family life should be equally shared.

Another way that traditional family therapists may exploit

women is by taking advantage of the fact that women are typically more adaptable to change than are men. Therapists often pay disproportionate attention to any efforts a man does make to change, while letting the woman accommodate on her own. Thus, his effort to become more expressive is seen by the therapist as the psychological equivalent of climbing Mount Everest, while her effort to enter the workplace after twenty years as a homemaker is seen as a privilege. At best, the traditional therapist may treat these two examples as representing equivalent effort, as if learning to cry and learning to be self-supporting are comparable tasks in a society that values money above all else.

In contrast, the feminist family therapist validates the husband's difficulty, pointing out that he has no training in the emotional expressiveness his family seeks, and that furthermore he will be going counter to the ethos of the workplace for developing it. At the same time the therapist suggests to the husband the potential rewards which might accrue to him for making such an effort within his family. The wife is validated regarding her fear of losing her clearly defined role of homemaker, along with the limited power that goes with it, for the slim chance of developing a positive identity as a worker in a society where women are still largely confined to low status service jobs earning less than two-thirds of what men earn. Management of the logistical, personal, and relational shifts attendant to her new position are given primary attention by the therapist.

An ironic twist to the husband/father's lack of involvement in the day to day life of the family is that, precisely because he has not been involved, he is often looked to by the traditional therapist as the one person who can now save the situation. Encouraging a father to take charge of a disruptive family conflict as an executive who will straighten out the mess his wife has created bespeaks a simplistic, functional view of roles in the family. In contrast, a feminist family therapist would understand such an intervention as conveying to the family that (1) mother has failed in her role, (2) father can do it better anyway, and (3) it takes an expert to persuade father to do what it takes to repair the situation. Therefore the feminist family therapist would want to design an intervention which emphasizes the importance of both parents' working to resolve the family conflict. Such an intervention would respect the position of the mother as the family's expert on child rearing. It would also speak to the benefits that would accrue to the father for increasing his involvement in the family's life, while noting that this change is not likely to be rewarded or even kindly viewed by the outside world (e.g., the workplace). If there is a commitment from both partners—from her that she is willing to share this responsibility and has other means available to her for expressing competence and from him that he is willing to pay the price in the workplace for the sake of being involved with his family—the intervention would be aimed at making parenting a shared responsibility. Such a model provides better insurance that children will be well nurtured than does making the mother entirely responsible for child rearing.

To summarize, the methodology of feminist family therapy practice includes (1) using self in the therapy as a model of human behavior not so constrained by gender stereotypes, (2) creating a process in which the use of such skills as validation, empowerment, and demystification increases their sense of having options for themselves and develops greater reciprocity among family members, (3) developing an analysis of gender roles in the family, (4) using this analysis to guide interactions with the family in ways that both challenge and free them from constricted, stereotypical patterns of behavior, and (5) drawing techniques from a variety of extant family therapy approaches, with full awareness of the gender consequences of these techniques.

Training

If therapy is to be feminist, training must be also. Presently, it is not. Obviously such a shift cannot occur by regarding feminism as an elective to be tacked on to what is—major changes must be made in the context, content, and process of our training programs.

Context

The system within which training is delivered must be organized in a way that does not reproduce the same oppressive and sexist arrangement which feminist family therapy intends to correct. To begin with, the program must have women in equal number with men in positions of authority as well as on the training staff. It must have the essential benefits sought in the business world: flexible scheduling, maternity and paternity leave, special supports for single parents and for older women entering the workforce. It must have feminist analysis as the first, not the second, language. It must have enlightened, respectful interaction as its hallmark.

To understand the importance of what we are saying, let us move from the level of context to the level of personal behavior. In their article on training, Caust, Libow, and Raskin refer to the "tendencies of women in general and female therapy trainees in particular to avoid confrontation, downplay their authority, and relate to supervisors in stereotyped, submissive ways as well as to use covert power strategies. . . . " (1981, p. 441). Although we agree with that observation, we want to make a different point than the authors made. Those behaviors are strategies of survival for subordinates. They are tendencies of women in general because women in general are subordinates. Where women are not subordinates (for example with their own children or in their roles as school teachers), they drop those behaviors and display their opposites. In other words, the ability to be authoritative and confrontive depends on the demand characteristics of the setting.

Contrary to the situation for women, virtually every setting is characterized by the expectation for men to act authoritative and confrontive. If those behaviors are desirable for women as therapists, the training setting must be reprogrammed, not the women. A woman's expectation of herself is a part of the change that must happen, but it is not the place to begin. First, the context must be made safe for women to exhibit a wider range of behavior, then it will emerge.

There are several factors complicating the effort to change the context of training. Present trainers must obtain special training before they can train differently. It takes much more than good intentions to accomplish the radical shift in consciousness and method that is necessary.

Another complication is that, as things now stand, the man-over-woman hierarchy overarches any particular hierarchy, such that even if a given woman has more designated authority than a given man or is designated as equal to him, she is commonly regarded as subordinate. Women supervisors, for example, are often treated as inferior to their male trainees, and women board members as inferior to male board members. So pervasive is this cultural ranking that it will not disappear in our training program by fiat, and will not disappear even if the other changes we have mentioned are put in place. The situation cannot be ignored, however. The hierarchy in the training program and in the larger institution housing the program needs to be taken as a continual and formal topic for study and discussion to specify its impact on the relationships, therapy, and training occurring under its sway.

Content

The program must teach feminist theory. Informing trainees about the patriarchal system under which we all grew and in which all families are embedded must be done explicitly and formally — waiting for personal "clicks" of awareness will not do. The training program has a responsibility to provide trainees with the concepts needed for performing the gender role analysis we described in the preceding section. Feminist scholarship provides rich resources (de Beauvoir, 1964; Chesler, 1972; Chodorow, 1978; Dinnerstein, 1976; Ehrenreich and English, 1978; French, 1985; Gilligan, 1982; Lerner, 1986; Miller, 1976; Oakley, 1974; Rich, 1976; Thorne, 1982); so also do women's literary works (Atwood, 1986; Bernikow, 1980; Brownmiller, 1984; Gilman, 1973b; Gould, 1976; Griffin, 1978; Griffith, 1984; Morgan, 1968; Pogrebin, 1983; Rich, 1986; Walker, 1982; Woolf, 1929).

There is further change in content to be accomplished. Trainers must engage with trainees in a joint and active effort to expose various aspects of favored family therapy theories as sexist. Many long-used training tapes, articles, and books which have seemed bedrock truth will now be used piecemeal; along with what good remains, we must demonstrate with these materials how pervasive, entrenched, and unquestioned have been the ways of sexist thinking. Although this critique is not yet completed, excellent material is found in Avis, in press; Avis, 1985; Bograd, 1984; Carter, 1986; Goldner, 1985a and b; James and McIntyre, 1983; Taggart, 1985. Reformations and new creations developing the application of feminist thought and action to family therapy theory, practice, and training are found in Carter, Papp, Silverstein, and Walters, 1984 a and b; Hare-Mustin, 1978; Libow, Raskin, and Caust, 1982; Margolin, Fernandez, Talovic, and Onorato, 1983; Simon, 1985; Wheeler, Avis, Miller, and Chaney, 1985.

We also propose to expand the content of the training that takes place during supervision of therapy, i.e., to add to what is held up for attention and observation. Some of our suggestions echo those given by Wheeler and her colleagues (1985). Components we consider most important are (1) to examine the relationship between the family and the therapist for the shape it is given by gender role expectations on the part of the family as well as on the part of the therapist; (2) to explore the division of labor, power, and rewards in the family as it is affected by gender bias and stereotyping; (3) to give specific attention to building for both men and women traditional womanly skills such as empathy, listening, supporting, and traditional manly skills such as giving clear directives, taking authoritative stances, displaying competence; and (4) to teach trainees to use their feelings instrumentally, that is, as indicators of the type of intervention needed or as diagnostic of key elements of the interactional process within the family or between family and therapist.

Finally, the content of personal work is different in training feminist family therapists. The trainees must examine stereotypical behavior in themselves and its consequences for themselves as well as for their client families. This exploration is best done by having the trainees discover and articulate these lessons as learned in their families of origin. It is of critical importance, however, to help them maintain the perspective that their families are a part of a larger social system in order to block any tendency to think that stereotyping has been invented by their mothers and fathers and is thus idiosyncratic to their own families.

Process

Respect is the primary defining feature of the process between trainers and trainees that we call for in feminist family therapy training. Since the word is general, we will be specific about certain applications.

—It is respectful to teach theory and method clearly rather than to make it confusing and inaccessible as a hierarchical marker.

—It is respectful to identify competencies, affirm improvement, support individuality, and be collaborative.

—It is disrespectful to have discussions threaded through with sexist jokes, sexist assumptions about a family's problem, and sexist language.

—It is disrespectful to use an interactive training style that is authoritarian, seductive, paternalistic, cute, hostile, or mystifying.

—It is not disrespectful in itself for trainees to display their work and for supervisors not to. It is not disrespectful in itself to regard the supervisors as knowing more than the trainees. The disrespect comes with the liberties supervisors often take to scold, tease, insult, or embarrass the trainees about their outlook, unique style, disagreement, or objection *because* of their higher position or greater knowledge—especially when that higher position has the extra accent of male supervisor, female trainee.

—It is not disrespectful in itself for a supervisor's approval to be required for advancement. What may be disrespectful is what it takes to obtain that approval. Is slavish devotion, exact copy, or unquestioning obedience the real agenda? Will original contributions and critical thinking be rewarded? How will supervisors view a creative, contributing, critical young woman? Is it a good idea for women to overcome what Caust, Libow, and Raskin (1981) describe as their "especially strong" motivation to win approval before they know the answer to that last question?

—It is not disrespectful in itself to phone-in messages to therapy or interrupt a session to guide a trainee. Some respectful ways for the supervisor to do so are: refrain from intervening long enough to allow the family and therapist to establish a relationship; ask permission before entering the room; either at the time or later, give a rationale for the timing and type of suggestion offered; show willingness to hear a difference and to experiment with alternatives.

Because the meanings and applications of respect are complicated, difficult to predict, and dangerous to address explicitly from an inferior position, we recommend that each supervisor/trainee team have consultants to their process to examine the sexual politics in the dyad. The consultants can be a working team, another supervisor/trainee pair, or an entire training group. We also recommend that trainees be able to work with both a man and a woman in the role of supervisor at some time during training.

We want to address some warnings directly to women who are now or may become trainees:

Beware of tokenism. Not every woman placed in a high position in training programs will be given the authority and acceptance necessary to carry out what seem to be her responsibilities. To the extent that such authority and acceptance are absent, your efforts to align with her or to watch her as a model will result in confusion for you. Similar confusion may arise for you from failure to note that not every woman trainer or author is a feminist.

Beware of assertiveness training. Efforts to teach you to change the way you make eye contact, hold yourself, show anger, or display power may be based on a model of how men do those things. Find out what exactly is objectionable about the way you are doing those things. Read Jean Baker Miller (1976) on power and anger to remind yourself that neither men nor women typically display power and anger in ways that are both effective and safe for humankind.

Beware of either/or thinking. Women do not need to stop being affiliative to be instrumental, or to stop being nurturant to be directive. The opportunity in training is to add skills, not drop some. Challenge everyone to think of ways to be both supportive and authoritative at the same moment.

Family therapy is, among other things, a moral endeavor. That is, family therapy is based on a vision of human life and of the environment best suited to produce and nourish human life. Women have had little part in creating that vision and scant opportunity to develop one they could recognize as their own. Feminists work for that opportunity, and for the next step: a way for that vision to have its day.

III
FEMINIST WORK, FEMINIST PROCESS

*This teacher tells us . . . we cannot rely on a
formula. She has made pot after pot over many
years and she says she still rides the unknown.
We must follow our hands . . . yield to the clay's
knowledge. She says every rule we have memo-
rized, the roughing and the wetting of edges, for
instance, . . . every law must yield to experience.
She says we must learn from each act, and no act
is ever the same.*

— *Susan Griffin,* Woman and Nature

THIS IS A CASE BOOK; subsequent chapters contain descriptions of
our work in therapy with selected families. The hope, of course, is
that what happened between us and these families might be instructive to other therapists when working with similar families.
How can we assume any similarity? The awesome singularity of
each individual person and of each individual family is the first
lesson worth knowing. Theories that mask this distinctiveness behind abstract, technical talk are a primary target of reformation.
However, it is equally important to examine the fundamental fact
of the social order and its imposition on the most personal aspects
of persons and families—their finances, their consciousness of self,
their expressions of sexuality, their manner of mothering and fa-
thering, and so on. This social order, this patriarchy, not only
intrudes everywhere but also spreads its disadvantages unevenly,
weighing more heavily on the weak and powerless than on the
highly placed and well-protected. We write of the similarity resulting from patriarchy and strive to preserve even in the writing

our sense of the uniqueness of each life we came to know in therapy.

The cases we have chosen to include in this book do not represent the range of cases family therapists work with in their practices. They are drawn from our own range, which is narrowed economically, socially, and racially by our region of the country, location in the city, arrangement of our practice, and various features of our selves and our training. From within this range, we have selected families in which the woman holds a stereotyped position. Typically therapists ignore her position, commonplace as it is (hence the stereotype) and are intrigued instead with the intricacies of the presented problem. We view her position as highly implicated in the problem and draw attention there.

The majority of the cases involve couples instead of families with children. This selection is also intentional. The presence of children in therapy inevitably pulls the focus to generational issues rather than gender issues. Since the purpose of this book is to highlight gender issues in therapy, we have chosen cases which lend themselves most clearly to such an analysis.

These cases, then, are meant to be instructive regarding women's stereotyped positions in particular and gender issues in general. We do not hold them out as representative of all lesbian couples, all single parent families, all corporate marriages, and so on. They are composites of families we have worked with and in that sense, speak for others.

Any report on a therapy case requires the author to select which facts, feelings, thoughts, and ideas to include. Our criterion for inclusion in the introductory presentation of each case was the difficulty we had with the therapy. We attempted to share what we as therapists had in mind as we worked with our clients, as well as what occurred in the sessions. Our purpose is to show the line of reasoning which led us to a stuck point, and then how we posed our problem to the consultation group.

For the cases reported in this book, we worked together according to our usual routine. On any given case, one or two of us works as the primary therapist(s), while the rest of us comprise the consultation team. We meet weekly to consult with each other. In a single meeting we might serve as the therapist on one case and consultant to two others. Usually we adopt the format of a case conference in which the therapist presents both the clinical material and her dilemma, and the group asks questions, suggests directions, and engages in dialogue with the therapist about how she might proceed. Occasionally we use videotapes, or one of us joins the therapist for a live consultation.

Need for consultation may manifest itself in different ways: as total blankness about how to proceed, as irritation with the client(s) for their pace, or as a wish that they would cancel their next appointment. Sometimes we feel stuck about a specific issue: Is this client interested in and ready to proceed with family of origin work? Have I established a working alliance with each spouse? Why do they never complete any of the assignments they agree to in session?

A consultation process parallels the therapy process. If the consultation presumes a rigid hierarchy between consultant and therapist, is strictly oriented to technique, and is disconnected from other contexts of the therapist's life, we can expect that therapy will also be hierarchical, oriented to technique, and blind to context. As feminists, we aspire to a different process for our consultation. First, we intend it to be collaborative. When we act as consultants, we do not take on extraordinary powers or status. Our purpose is not to make the therapist work in our image, but to facilitate the development of her *own* best style of work. Second, our consultations are highly personal. We attempt to create an environment in which the therapist can discover and examine her own blind spots and biases. Questions about her connection to the issues her clients bring are therefore a central feature of our consultations. The answers are personal, but they indicate common dilemmas for the feminist family therapist and therefore have become the pitfalls described at the end of each chapter.

Finally, the questions we ask as consultants, indeed our entire view of the case, are distinctively shaped by our commitment to making feminism an explicit part of the context of therapy. Regardless of the particulars of the case, there are certain questions which we regard as crucial to a feminist consultation and always keep before us: How are our clients understanding gender, and how is that understanding limiting their ability to solve their problem? How are we understanding gender, and how is that understanding affecting our conception of the clients' problems? What gender bias is contained in the theory we are using and how is it hindering the therapeutic process?

For ease of presentation in this book, we report on the consultation in one or two sections of each chapter. Actually, we consulted on some of these cases more than a dozen times. Similarly, we collect into the analysis section of each chapter an elaboration on various points that arose for us in the consultation process, including our critique of family therapy.

The analysis of each presented case grows out of the particulars of the case, but quickly becomes general in the sense that we examine relevant social patterns, popular opinion, and professional theories. Still, the analysis remains personal because social patterns, popular opinion, and professional theories shape as well as reflect the way people live and the way people interpret how they live. Those personal issues of living and meaning are our abiding interest.

There are various places to stand when analyzing human events: in the biologist's laboratory, at the fundamentalist's pulpit, on the Democrat's platform, over the economist's books, behind the psychoanalyst's couch, with the family therapist's team, and others. The choice of where to stand is critical because it determines the concepts and values to be used for the analysis. The place we long stood was with family therapy, but the ground kept giving way beneath us.

All these positions rest on a foundation that is either feminist ground or sexist (and may also be racist, classist, and so on). We have chosen to stand on feminist ground and the view from that perspective has shown us that everything that we have taken to be true—both from family therapy and from other disciplines—has to be re-examined, rethought, and reinvented. Our analyses are therefore long, gathered primarily into one section of each chapter, but appearing throughout because analysis is continuous. Feminism must be thorough precisely because everything that is not examined remains sexist.

Following our analysis, we set forth the goals which guided our work with each case and a brief description of ways to meet each goal. Sometimes the plan we have written contains approaches we ended up not using. We include them because we want to emphasize that there are a number of ways to get from here to there; working as if there is one right assignment takes a therapist away from active contact with the clients.

The goals, of course, emerged from our understanding of a given problem and our values about what contributes to the best living possible. Our understanding of the problem and our values are explicated in sections on Consultation and Analysis; the goals are pointed restatements. Clearly, these were *our* goals for the family we were seeing. Still, we are committed to a collaborative process, and we presented our goals to our clients through discussion, suggested reading, rationale for homework, metaphor, and so on. To the extent that our goals for the family sufficiently matched the family's own or provided an appealing alternative to the family's own, our work was able to proceed.

At times our clients did not accept our goals because we had moved too far from their experience and become utopian in our desires for them. We do call for broad and fundamental change. Certainly in contrast to goals such as "fewer arguments per week," ours are utopian. The implication for us is not to relax the effort but to prepare for more disappointment than would come if we scaled down our vision. Scaling down would be eminently sensible if only the vision were not so important, and arrangements were not so damaging.

Next we describe the therapy. This description is at best an approximation, much like writing a story of any personal experience, so to read it as a literal account leads off in the wrong direction. We need to acknowledge that therapy is often mysterious. It is an encounter where more happens than we can know or tell, and more even than a tape can faithfully preserve since we can never know exactly what we were thinking and we most assuredly do not know what our clients were thinking. All we can report is what we think transpired. Conversation rides on many assumptions about meaning between participants, most of which are unspoken and unverified.

Our reporting involved making choices, and selecting what we believed were the important issues. Our purpose is to highlight gender issues: How does the therapist assist this family to see themselves and each other in ways that are not constricted by gender? How does she interact with them in ways that enable them to behave other than stereotypically? Issues not distinctly feminist — for example, stress management, engaging the family, handling missed appointments — are not addressed.

We think we know what helped, and this is what we report. We think we know what did not help and we report that too. We do not convey here what brought tears to our eyes or made us laugh out loud. We have said elsewhere in this book that the encounter itself—the relationship between therapist and family, therapist and client—is critical, and our writing has not captured that. To do so, we would need to sing a song, write a poem, or paint a picture.

We close each clinical report with the pitfalls that await a feminist family therapist in approaching the issues raised in each case. These were identified during our consultations with one another. Some we discovered because we had fallen in; others because we had chanced to look before we leaped.

By and large, the pitfalls are of two kinds. One kind reflects the likely ways that sexism may intrude on our understanding or intervention. There remains an unreconstructed part in all of us with reflexive responses which demonstrate that we were born and bred under patriarchy. These responses impede our clients' progress towards liberation. No matter how deep our commitment to feminism and how thorough our efforts to purge ourselves of sexism, some effects of social conditioning will persist. We need one another as consultants in order to stay alert to this influence.

The other kind of pitfall reflects the likely ways of being overcome by missionary zeal. Some issues or interactions in therapy strike so directly at the heart of the injury and inequity perpetrated by patriarchy as to ignite our passions and righteous indignation. Responses such as rage, lecturing, rescuing, debating, and preaching all have a place, but therapy is not it. Again, we need one another as consultants in order to stay alert.

We use different narrative voices for the different sections of our clinical chapters. We have the therapist report the therapy sessions, using "I," or "we" on those few occasions when there are two. In the consultation sections, the team speaks as "we" to report the conferences with the therapist. As mentioned earlier, the person acting as therapist in one chapter becomes part of the consultation team in the next. For the analysis section, we make a more formal presentation as authors and do not use a personal referent despite our personal involvement and commitment.

IV
THE CORPORATE MARRIAGE

*Men in America do not have much
time for love. Severe division of labor
keeps the sexes apart, and standards
of business discourage intimacy.*

— *Alexis de Tocqueville,* Democracy
in America

A CORPORATE MARRIAGE is a socioeconomic arrangement in which
the husband holds high status within the corporate world and is
the sole producer of income for the family, while the wife manages
house, children, and self in a manner that eases the way for his
success and displays it according to the prevailing fashion. In such
marriages, the culture of the corporation exerts such enormous
influence over the marriage as to give it a distinctive shape. We
include such a case in this book because we believe that the corporate context places constraints on marriage that are highly gendered, and that the incidence of such marriages is frequent enough
to warrant special attention by family therapists.

The husbands are bright, successful executives who are highly
identified with the work ethic. The wives are bright, educated
homemakers, usually without significant work experience, highly
identified with their roles as wife and mother. The standards of
performance they use as guides are prescribed for them by the
corporate circle (Kanter, 1977). Both husband and wife are quintessential consumers (i.e., they have the best cars, membership in

the right country club, and a home that is a showcase with all the latest technology) (Clark, Nye, and Gecas, 1978).

Among those who seek therapy, the relationship between these marital partners (frequently of twenty years or more) can be characterized as devitalized (Skolnick, 1983). It is as if all the life inside and between these individuals has been drained and only skeletons of their roles and functions remain. Extreme role differentiation prevails, not only concerning the provider/homemaker split, but also in the traits presumed to accompany it. She is to be nurturant, dependent, and passive; he is to be strong, independent, and rational. This differentiation is highly valued by the couple and carries moral weight: she *should not* take on a career; he *should not* be bothered with domestic troubles.

The distribution of power in these marriages is weighted heavily in the husband's favor and wives do not typically challenge this dominant/subordinate structure. Dominants do not permit questions to be raised about their rights and actions; subordinates dare not raise them. Thus conflicts rarely become explicit.

An adequate description of the corporate marriage requires attention to one more major partner. Because the corporation itself requires and receives such enormous amounts of devotion, loyalty, time, and energy, it is useful to consider it the organizing principle of the marriage. In many respects, the corporation prescribes the life of the couple and reinforces the dominant/subordinate structure of husband and wife.

Visions and promises. Corporate marriage holds out the promise of graceful living in the *House Beautiful* tradition. Desired and expected benefits include financial security, social position, beautiful home, travel, and happiness. Everyone is supposed to win. The corporation has a hard-working employee prepared to do its bidding and kept free to do so by his well-rewarded wife. She is to find fulfillment in being a good wife, mother, and homemaker; he in being successful at work and in providing for his family. This vision gains further appeal by being stamped with widespread social approval.

It is inevitable that the vision does not deliver all it promises. The husband, well-socialized to expect fulfillment through providing, labors long and hard but waits in vain for the meaning that can only come from loving and sharing. The wife, well-socialized to expect fulfillment through enabling, labors long and hard but waits in vain for the meaning that can only come through public recognition and recompense for one's own work. Neither husband nor wife understands the consequences of their arrangement with each other and with the corporation: to forego autonomy and self-direction as a couple, and to let graceful living replace intimate living as the primary reward of the marriage.

Coming to therapy. The various presenting symptoms that bring other types of families into therapy also bring corporate families (e.g., wife's depression or husband's alcoholism, or vice versa). Sometimes, an adolescent is the catalyst for therapy. In that instance, we see a pattern of behavior that exactly counters the major themes of the parent of the same sex. For example, the daughter may take a stand of exaggerated independence, which is most flagrantly depicted in early sexual activity. The son may take a stand of exaggerated irresponsibility, hugging the line between success and failure in following the requirements of school, household, and law.

Whether the husband and wife come jointly to have the identified patient treated or only one partner comes for individual therapy, the arrangement of the corporate marriage itself is not recognized by the couple as the problem and therefore is not presented as such. The original visions and promises are not questioned, the original contract is not faulted, and the original definition of roles is not challenged. Instead, dissatisfaction, which is characteristically without open conflict, centers on the circumstance that one or both parties are not fulfilling their part of the bargain.

Linda and Dick

Dick and Linda, an attractive couple in their mid-forties, were married for twenty years when they sought therapy. At initial presentation, Dick looked embarrassed and shy while Linda appeared confident, acting almost too familiar with me. Therapy was initiated by Dick, who was concerned that he no longer knew how Linda felt about him. Dick complained that he could no longer see in her behavior signs that he mattered to her. Linda expressed surprise at his being unaware of her caring but maintained she would be glad to provide whatever signs he needed if he would just list them. Dick's annoyance at having to tell Linda rather than having her already know began to emerge here as the first among several examples of the "be spontaneous" paradox which the couple displayed.

The first session was a vivid portrayal of the corporate marriage. Dick, a fifteen-year veteran with a multi-national corporation, had been for the last three years doing field work for approximately two weeks of every month. He felt good about his job and was grateful to have it. Linda, a homemaker with two children, one in high school and one in college, was pleased with her beautiful home, her children, and her friends. She reported with pride that she was well adjusted to Dick's work schedule, just as she had become adjusted to previous demands from Dick's employment, including several intercontinental moves: "It's what you have to do. Ask me anything about how to move a household in less than two weeks."

It seemed apparent that Linda's way of adjusting was the very thing that Dick was now interpreting as not caring. During the moves, Linda busied herself with making a new home for her family and finding outlets for herself in hobbies and volunteer work. When I asked Dick and Linda how they attempted to reconnect with each other after each move, neither could recall what they had attempted, if anything.

In subsequent sessions, Linda appeared to be a willing client, but not really involved in the therapy. She seemed to be there primarily to demonstrate good faith and to prove that she was a loyal wife. Because Dick said little more than he had in the initial session, I first intervened by assisting him with the words he lacked to articulate his feelings to Linda. In their past interactions, Linda's use of psychological jargon had intimidated Dick, rendering him almost speechless. My first intervention with Linda was to help her become reacquainted with her feelings: "Some women in your situation might have felt very angry, sad, or hopeless." Admitting such feelings was particularly difficult for Linda because her presentation of self was so wedded to her ability to adjust.

I gave a positive connotation to Dick's and Linda's behaviors as indicating real interest in each other over the years of their marriage but shown from too great a distance. Dick and Linda agreed with my interpretation about them and seemed receptive to the goal of increasing their level of intimacy and their effectiveness at communication. Neither one, however, made any substantial move toward accomplishing this goal. Interventions in session and assignments for home were virtually halted before they began, usually by Dick's unwillingness to proceed. Dick's confused reluctance looked like shyness, Linda's superficial participation looked like distance. I felt shut out by both of them.

I then constructed a new frame, attempting to convince Dick and Linda that the corporation was the culprit and their common enemy, so to speak—that in fact their lives had been directed by the capriciousness of the corporation. This stance, however, left no place for Dick's loyalty and gratitude (not to mention his identification with his company) and so was not perceived by him as empathic. Linda was not ready to lay blame at the company's door.

An interesting shift took place at the next session when I asked the couple how a homework assignment had gone. Dick began to assert (quietly but forcefully) that he liked himself as he was and that Linda was clearly lacking self-confidence and was unhappy. For her part, all Linda could say was that she doubted her intelligence and her ability to manage the small businesses she had attempted, but that she was not unhappy. I wanted to avoid a picture that made Linda the client and Dick the man who brought her in, so I continued in the next few sessions to try to find concerns in which both would continue to be the "client" and participate. Despite these attempts Dick initiated the termination of therapy, saying that he had no interest in changing his behavior and that the remaining task was for Linda to gain self-confidence so that he would not be set up as her father. Dick said that he hoped Linda would work this out in a therapy of her own.

From my perspective, Dick was unwilling to do more than initiate therapy and set the stage. He hardly struggled with his own behavior. I assumed that he would not be making an appointment for himself, and that Linda would only initiate individual therapy to help her deal with Dick's lack of responsiveness in the marriage. Besides recognizing this case as unfinished, I was also aware of my dilemma. To view the problem strictly as a manifestation of the idiosyncrasies within the marital relationship would have been ignoring the corporation's control and intrusion. Yet any attempt I made to expand the context of the problem to include the corporation was rebuffed by the couple.

Consultation

The therapist sought a consultation to analyze the case and to develop a plan for future work, should either member of the couple return to therapy. We (as consultants) first addressed the locus of the problem within the system. Although the content of the marital therapy had focused on the interaction between Dick and Linda, the therapist continued to see the corporation as a third troubling element. The drawback to this definition of the problem was that it offered no therapeutic leverage, however much sense it made. The corporation had not come for therapy. While acknowledging that corporate culture was an essential part of the context in which the marriage had failed to function, we agreed with the therapist that defining the problem within the marital system would offer the greater therapeutic advantage.

The therapist still needed to grapple with the differences between each partner's definition of the problem. She had rightly resisted Dick's interpretation of Linda as "the problem." The entire culture supports the idea that marriage is the responsibility of women. For the therapist to subscribe to such an idea would have put her in the position of supporting an oppressive cultural myth. This conceptualization would have limited the therapist's options just as severely as accepting the corporation as the problem would have. Clearly, Dick had also participated in the devitalization of this marriage.

Another obstacle to defining a solvable problem for this couple was that the therapist held assumptions about a marriage contract that differed from those of her clients. The therapist believed that the marital relationship should be constructed on a foundation of caring and love, and its goal should be to sustain intimacy. Dick and Linda seemed to support this value overtly; however, they behaved as if intimacy could be established and maintained simply by agreeing that she would provide a home, children, and sexual services and that he would provide money. The therapist was pursuing a goal for her clients that they could not embrace for themselves. This approach accounted for the lack of success in engaging the couple in exercises to enhance communication and intimacy. The therapist was pushing for substance while they were desperately clinging to form.

The form of the marriage stemmed from the original economic agreement. Dick believed that Linda *owed* him love because he provided her with financial security. Her task, as he saw it, was to make him feel desirable and lovable. For her part it was vital that Linda believe she did love Dick, in order to avoid feeling that she was selling her affection. It was thus very difficult for her to acknowledge any lack of feeling for her husband, either to herself or the therapist. The fulfillment of her needs depended on her satisfying *his* needs. Indeed, in consultation we speculated that not knowing her own needs (for intimacy, recognition, competence) was necessary for the arrangement to continue.

The therapist suspected that Linda had learned early not to express her needs or disappointments to Dick and then convinced herself that she had none, thereby colluding with her husband in her own mystification. They both saw her doubts and fears as evidence of *her* insecurity, never of his insufficiency or of the flaws inherent in the arrangement.

Therapy with Linda and Dick demonstrated several interpersonal issues that commonly arise in the treatment of a corporate marriage. The relationship between Linda and the therapist was marked with a high degree of ambivalence on Linda's part. To her, as a corporate wife, the therapist represented both a model of the independent woman she wished to be and an implicit accusation of the waste and irrelevance of her chosen life. The strategy that Linda used to control her anxiety regarding the therapist paralleled an aspect of her relationship with Dick. Rather than engage in direct confrontation, Linda tried subtly to demonstrate her superiority to the therapist by making comments to the therapist about her personal appearance ("Nice color, but you really shouldn't wear your skirts so long, it makes you look shorter."); personal life ("You're going to Paris in July? But it will be so crowded!"); and even intimations that the therapist was not quite current in her reading of the literature ("You haven't read this book yet? Oh, but you simply must!").

Linda also tried to engage the therapist in a coalition against Dick, frequently alluding to their common gender or shared interest in psychology. Winks, knowing smiles, or technical language were used to underscore these similarities and the corresponding distance from Dick. Any plan for future treatment would have to include ways of avoiding such maneuvers.

From the therapist's perspective, Linda had become the quintessential corporate wife. When she was young, she was courted with the promise of success that she believed Dick could obtain and that she knew she could not secure for herself. She did her part to manage the home while he was slaying corporate dragons. As the years advanced and the children were too old and independent to provide shared ground for them anymore, Linda had less and less in common with Dick. Originally, she had agreed to separate spheres as the way to create a financially successful and secure family; now she found that she and her husband were distant galaxies away from each other.

Dick matched the therapist's stereotype of a corporate man: he subscribed to the values of the corporation uncritically, believed his wife owed him devotion because he supported her financially, and demonstrated no interest in and little ability for sharing his life emotionally. This situation challenged the therapist and although we knew it would be difficult, we nonetheless underscored the need for her to connect with Dick by finding some positive, non-stereotypic aspect of his life. In addition, we suggested that the therapist avoid dealing with Dick in ways Linda had. The therapist, like Linda, had tried to help Dick with his inability to articulate his point of view. Eventually, like Linda, the therapist became frustrated with this effort.

During the consultation session, considerable time was spent discussing whether the therapist could and should accept the terms of her clients' marital contract. Dick and Linda were staying together primarily for the sake of maintaining their life-style. Caring, affection, and respect were secondary. Because this contract represented the antithesis of the therapist's notion about marriage, she had to search for some aspect of the marriage that she could support in order to respect her clients' choice to remain together. We suggested that individual sessions with Linda and Dick might be useful in helping the therapist understand and empathize with their marital bargain. If the therapist could get a stronger sense of the positive aspects Dick and Linda saw in their bargain, she would be better able to help the couple lessen the blame towards each other and feel more responsible and powerful.

Analysis

Two strong interacting variables create the corporate marriage: the corporation itself, and the rigid division of labor, expectations, and values that comprise male and female gender roles. The ideology of both corporation and gender role has a profound impact on the marriage.

Identification with the corporation. Most men in this society obtain their sense of self primarily through their work. What is particular to the corporate man is that his identification is with an institution which is an embodiment of power. As a result, he too feels powerful, and all the perks provided him by the corporation serve to reinforce that perception. In return, he is expected to give deference, loyalty, and conformity to the ethos of the corporation.

Two major consequences follow. First, these men spend most of their waking hours acting out the corporate style: denying feelings, maintaining control, and following blueprints for their behavior.[1] When they arrive home, they cannot suddenly become the vulnerable, trusting, expressive persons that intimate relations demand. Second, corporate men, in the name of their job and in line with their sense of importance, take the major part in marital decision-making. The higher they rise in prestige and income, the greater their power in the marriage (Conklin, 1981).

As Jessie Bernard (1972) has suggested, there are two marriages in the corporate couple: his and hers, separate but not equal. His is a simpler story, though by no means without casualties and losses.

---

[1]C. Wright Mills captured the sense of the corporate setting in his mock charge to the young executive: "Between decision and execution, between command and obedience, let there be reflex. Be calm, judicious, rational; groom your personality and control your appearance; make business a profession. Develop yourself. Write a memo; hold a conference with men like you . . . nod gravely to the girls in the office; say hello to the men; and always listen carefully to the ones above" (1951, p. 81).

Hers is far more complex, perhaps because she has so much more riding on it. "Marriage," observed Charlotte Perkins Gilman at the turn of the century, "is the one road to fortune for women" (1973a, p. 582). Marriage may be many things for men, but it is certainly not the one road to fortune. Though dated, Gilman's observation still holds an important measure of truth: generally it is men who make fortunes, not women; and if a woman is interested in fortune she will generally need to marry a "successful" man. While Dick, as a youth, was planning *what* he would achieve and attain, Linda, as a youth, was planning *whom* she would achieve and attain.

His marriage. In the corporate family, the husband is the provider whose income and status establish a standard and style of living for his dependents. He may help out with the children or assist in the kitchen, but it is abundantly clear that he is doing "extra work," more than his share. Given the corporation's demands for long hours, out-of-town travel, and transfers, the husband may be more appropriately characterized as married to the corporation than to the wife. Nevertheless, numerous studies have demonstrated that marriage is good for men. Compared to unmarried men, married men have far better health; they show fewer serious symptoms of psychological distress; they live longer; they are happier; and they can assume, with statistical confidence, that their marriage will be an asset to both their career and their earning power.

Her marriage. More wives than husbands report marital frustrations and problems, and more wives initiate counseling and divorce. Compared to married men and unmarried women, married women show much more evidence of poor emotional health (e.g., phobic reactions, depression, passivity, and anxiety). Jesse Bernard has suggested that marriage introduces such absolute discontinuities into women's lives "as to constitute genuine emotional health hazards" (1972, p. 37).

The metamorphosis of a woman into a wife involves a redefinition of the self and an active reshaping of her personality to conform to the wishes, needs, and demands of her husband. She holds no real power, makes more concessions and adjustments than her husband, and is often reconciled, not happy. If she finds herself complaining, she has all of her training and her present society (friends, family, magazines) reminding her that her life is good: something must be wrong with her if she is so unhappy. Confusion and despair result to the point that she does not know what she wants. Not knowing what she wants is perceived as further evidence of her personal inadequacy.

Nothing in the marital or legal system respects the wife's work in her home as employment. As Gilman observed, "The labor which the wife performs in the household is given as part of her functional duty, not as employment" (1973a, p. 573). The wife is not legally entitled to any share in the family assets which she has indirectly helped the husband earn. Since she is denied direct legal action against her husband unless she files for divorce, her generally understood "right to support" is an empty phrase (Krauskopf, 1977).

Many women stay in less-than-satisfying corporate marriages for the same reasons women stay in other marriages. They understand their limited options. They believe they should be appreciative of what they are given (which is often quite generous in economic terms). They have learned to accept and adjust to the requirements and demands of marriage. Finally, they too have become transformed by the corporation, and all that it provides: status, prestige, and physical comforts.

Costs to the husband. Men pay a high price for the power, status, and money gained from their position in the corporate structure. There are daily struggles, uncertainties, disappointments, and competitiveness that are not only difficult to manage but also are precursors to or even producers of various "executive illnesses," most notably cardiovascular disease (Friedman and Rosenman, 1981). Other health hazards associated with high management positions are addiction to tobacco and alcohol and a higher suicide rate compared to women of the same age.

Absence from home, little involvement with family members, and development of interests quite different from their wives' interests are common circumstances for corporate men which tend to break down marriage and family life (Seidenberg, 1973). More importantly, the executive role fosters the development of personality traits that are inconsistent with successful family life. To blend into the corporate team, the executive learns to narrow his range of responsiveness and to shut down personal spontaneity and creativity (Bartolome, 1972; Maccoby, 1976). This emotional stunting makes it virtually impossible to maintain an intimate marital relationship.

Costs to the wife. Heavy as the costs are to the man, the woman typically pays more. "Corporations have been less than kind to women. Their cruelty has been as much out of *machismo* as malice" (Seidenberg, 1973, p. vii). Wives are treated as playthings and servants by both the company and the company man. In a study offering executives the opportunity to describe the role of corporate wife, researchers found that the terms used were those ordinarily used for receptionists or other subordinate employees. None of the participating executives mentioned such traits as intelligence, independence, or resourcefulness. In fact, all agreed that the ideal corporate wife should specifically not be involved in any aspect of the corporate world that would require the use of her mind (as reported in Seidenberg, 1973, pp. 72–74).

Because her husband is gone so much of the time, the corporate wife has virtually exclusive responsibility for care of the children. The isolation that can result from this focus is often lessened by involvement in community service; however, frequent moves required by the corporation result in a loss of credentials, contacts, and status — the very benefits earned by and necessary for rewarding community service. Many corporate wives use housework to fill the emptiness that results from their separation from resources of culture, community, and opportunity for growth. Because housework cannot perform that function, corporate wives come to know as primary features of their lives loneliness, borrowed identity, and vicarious achievement.

Much of the cost to the wives derives from the inequality built into the arrangement of the marriage. It is impossible to have an egalitarian relationship in the home when the two partners are so plainly unequal in the world. Neither one forgets the values of the public sphere when dealing with one another in the personal sphere.

Costs to the society. Although there are numerous costs to society, we have limited ourselves to mentioning two. The first concerns the corporate culture. The definition of success that prevails in our society matches the corporate definition of success: climbing high on the hierarchical ladder, making lots of money, wielding economic and decision-making powers over others, and enjoying a life of conspicuous consumption. As long as this definition holds and the corporations that embody it have the influence they do, we will continue to live in an environment marked by political manipulation rather than consensual cooperation, by an emphasis on instrumentality uncorrected by expressive and spiritual values, and by the equation of the successful life with the monied life.

The second and related thought concerns the rigid role differentiation that is so clearly articulated, demonstrated, and blessed in the corporate marriage. This feature contributes to the fact that neither the men nor their wives develop rich and flourishing personalities. To underscore this point, we draw from Margaret Mead:

> Throughout history, the more complex activities have been defined and re-defined, now as male, now as female, now as neither, sometimes as drawing equally on the gifts of both sexes, sometimes as drawing differentially on both sexes. When an activity to which each could have contributed — and probably all complex activities belong in this class — is limited to one sex, a rich differentiated quality is lost from the activity itself. . . . Once a complex activity is defined as belonging to one sex, the entrance of the other sex into it is made difficult and compromising (1949, p. 372).

Society's cost, then, is not only found by summing the losses in the individual lives of corporate husbands and wives, but also by envisioning the contributions that are *not* made in the home, office, or community, because they are disallowed.

Treatment

Goals

At the time of our meeting, the therapist did not expect to see Dick and Linda again for therapy. Nevertheless, we developed goals for treatment and a plan for accomplishing the goals in case

Dick and Linda did return, and as a guide for our future work with corporate couples. Our underlying goals were:

(1) to make explicit the shaping force of the corporate culture on Dick, on Linda, and on their marriage;
(2) to facilitate the exploration of options for them as a couple, and for Dick and Linda as individuals;
(3) to examine the consequences of each option;
(4) to ensure that both Dick and Linda feel empowered to decide the best course; and
(5) to promote mutuality.

Plan

Context. Family therapy literature has largely ignored the effect of the corporate context on the family life of executives. Only one article directly addresses the special circumstances of the corporate family (Gulotta, 1981). In contrast to the approach we are recommending here, Gulotta explicitly discourages family therapists from discussing the constraints that the corporation places on the family's life and also admonishes therapists not to attempt changing the husband's level of involvement with his family. By default, the responsibility for change falls to the wife, who does not even have the privilege of understanding the limitations of her power. From a feminist perspective, such a stance is inevitably mystifying and unfairly burdensome to the wives in these families.

In planning how to help Dick and Linda understand the context of their marriage, we knew we had to avoid painting the corporation as the culprit, thereby prompting a defense of the corporation. To go a different route, the therapist could personalize the Analysis section by teaching and connecting a little at a time as points become personally relevant to Dick and Linda. For example, the therapist could wonder about individual and joint complaints as consequences of requirements of the corporation and/or as the price paid for listed benefits.

Options. Expectations about one's life are based on gender stereotypes made further specific by role. Thus, the options that Dick would list for himself are limited by his view of what a man can do, as well as by what a corporate executive can do. Linda is similarly limited in her vision and in addition has incorporated the lesson taught to many women, i.e., that paying attention to what she wants, much less speaking about it aloud, is not a legitimate undertaking for women. Helping Dick and Linda consider more options in their search for solutions requires that the therapist challenge the ways they are accustomed to thinking about themselves. Methods of strategic therapy would be useful here, especially exaggeration and restraining techniques.

Consequences. The consequences of each option are very different for the corporate husband and wife. Divorce, for example, would raise the level of Dick's economic life-style and not alter his social status significantly. In contrast, Linda's life-style would deteriorate and her social status would vanish. The consequences of staying in the marriage also differ. The therapist needs to help Dick and Linda evaluate consequences separately, but within hearing of the other.

Empowerment. Linda, like many women, is used to letting her fate be decided by her husband rather than deciding it for herself. Dick, like many men, is used to seeing himself as a responsible party and is confident in that role. His model of decision-making, however, is limited to competitiveness and nonnegotiation. For both Dick and Linda, a primary avenue for assistance would be the behavior of the therapist—providing empathy, listening respectfully, validating concerns, and exploring new avenues opened through patience and questioning. The other primary avenue would be a commitment to mutuality.

Mutuality. If Dick and Linda choose to remain in the marriage, we would like to see them committed to mutuality. Both should offer respectful listening and be alert to unfairness. Both should use skills to negotiate differences and experience their relationship as strong enough to bear the conflict required to grow into a better arrangement. Both should challenge the idea that the person who makes the most money in the corporate world deserves the greatest voice in the personal world of marital decision-making. Given the characteristics of the corporate marriage, this ideal may not even be adopted by Dick and Linda, let alone achieved. Still, we believe it is a disservice to them not to hold it before them.

Dick and Linda

A few months after marital therapy ended, Linda made an appointment for further therapy, saying she was sad, hopeless, and lethargic. Dick continued to oppose any further treatment for himself. Over a period of several months, I encouraged Linda to consider her options and she vacillated between polarized solutions (either becoming the "total woman" or asking Dick to leave). I suggested that she take her time and consider more moderate solutions such as assessing whether Dick could or would meet her expectations, and finding other ways of satisfying her emotional needs for support and closeness. As her relationship with me developed further, she came to see herself as someone with a right to more than a reconciled existence. She admitted that intimacy and communication were what she wanted with Dick and decided to risk being the initiator. I cautioned her that once she asked Dick for what she wanted he might, in fact, leave. Linda decided to try anyway.

With some coaching from me, Linda put the following question to Dick: Is there something that I can do that would make you feel responsive to me? To her surprise, he answered no. When she asked him why he could stay married to her, he had no response. After several more weeks, Linda informed him that she saw no reason to continue living with someone who showed her no regard. Dick moved his belongings that day. Several months later, Linda learned that he had been having an affair with his secretary for some time and had probably been involved with her during their marital therapy.

Over the next year, I worked with Linda as she took the first tentative steps towards creating a future for herself. She is now divorced, working for an interior design group, and has joined a support group for separated and divorced people at her church. Her definition of herself has expanded far beyond what she knew as a corporate wife and she reports that she likes herself very much.

Dick has married his secretary, whom he was seeing while he

was married to Linda. In the corporate world where men spend more time with their secretaries than with their wives, where required travel provides a conducive setting, where "female entertainers" are often used to help land customers and reward extra effort, and where the corporation thinks very little of wives except to advance their husbands' careers, it should be no surprise to us that Dick was unfaithful. It is, but it should not be.

Although Dick and Linda's solution was to end their relationship, other couples might opt to preserve their relationship while decreasing their discomfort. Such a choice is exemplified by another corporate couple, Jay and Frieda.

Frieda and Jay

Like Dick and Linda, Jay and Frieda had been married for almost two decades when they first sought therapy. Jay was an engineer who held a management position with a large petrochemical company. Frieda was a homemaker and an active volunteer in the community. The couple came to therapy bringing their 16-year-old son who was doing poorly in school and had been suspended for drug possession. The son's behavior improved steadily as his parents began to discuss the many small, unresolved conflicts in their relationship. By the end of the sixth session, the son announced that he did not think he needed to continue coming to sessions, and his parents and I agreed.

Marital therapy focused on the basic issues of the marriage: its coolness, lack of vitality, and inability to meet the couple's needs. Each spouse held a distinctly different view of the problem. Jay believed that he was as involved in his marriage as he had ever been and that Frieda's complaints had only begun when their youngest child reached high school. His proposed solution was that Frieda involve herself in more outside activities, such as her volunteer work. He also suggested that their home was due for major remodeling and that this was a project at which Frieda would excel. Frieda admitted that some of her problem was boredom, but she asserted that it had always been one of their dreams to slow down the pace of their lives after the children were grown. Jay was reneging on this agreement and had in fact taken on new challenges and greater responsibilities at work in the past two years. Still they were clear about how committed they were to their marriage. Each acknowledged a deeply held belief that everything would be all right in the marriage if only the other would change.

Based on my consultants' recommendations, I wanted to place the marriage in its corporate context. To enhance empathy between the spouses, I strove to emphasize the *differences* in their situations—the difference between working for a corporation and being married to someone who works there; the difference between having a "kept woman" and being one. In a general way, I engaged the couple in a discussion about how her marriage was different from his, and how easy it had become to see these differences as signs of failure, rejection, and accusation. Their initial reaction to this analysis was a mixture of relief at feeling understood and suspicion that the acknowledgment of these differences was somehow going to lead to greater separation and more animosity between them. However as I continued to validate *both* their positions, they began to deal with each other in a less blaming, less pathologizing way. Each was able to hear the other's pain without feeling at fault.

This shift was probably more difficult for Jay, who felt terribly disloyal acknowledging that his company had contributed in any negative way to the quality of his life. In discussing this subject with him, I was careful to emphasize my position that while the corporation was not a useful scapegoat in this marriage, it was and would continue to be a constraining factor in the solutions that Jay and Frieda might apply to their marital problems.

For this therapy to be successful, I realized that I would have to find a way to respect the couple's value system, even if it was very different from my own. In addition, I needed to get beyond the perfected public images that Frieda and Jay presented to the world, to develop a sense of their identities apart from their familiar roles. To accomplish both of these goals, I scheduled for each spouse several individual sessions with content ranging from their individual family histories to current everyday life. Establishing a relationship with each spouse as an individual proved to be invaluable in actualizing subsequent therapeutic goals.

Once therapy had neutralized the differences Jay and Frieda saw in each other, I focused on helping the couple evaluate the costs and benefits attached to the options of staying in or dissolving the marriage. After twenty years of marriage, Frieda's identity was so embedded in her roles as wife and mother that it was hard for her to imagine a satisfying life outside of marriage. Frieda, who saw women friends go through divorces, was well aware of the significant loss of financial security and social status a divorce would mean, and responded to the thought with paralyzing anxiety. While Jay *could* envision a tolerable single life devoted to his corporate career, he could not imagine a personal life apart from Frieda. He believed that he would never again invest the same sort of emotional energy in a relationship that he felt he had invested in his marriage. Inertia, as he put it, was working against him.

Over the years of marriage, each spouse had become invisible to the other, no longer seen as unique, interesting, or attractive. I used the technique of talking to one spouse about the positive qualities of the other as a means of jarring these permanent, fixed perceptions. For example, I casually asked Jay how it felt to have such a charming and attractive wife, and commented to Frieda about what a good dresser her husband was, or how physically fit he looked. Each partner was also instructed to ask friends and family members for perceptions about the spouse, and to think up things to say to or do for each other that would be surprising, or out of character. The cumulative effect of such interventions was to make Frieda and Jay each a little less certain that the other was an "open book."

Once Frieda and Jay made the decision to stay together and try to make the marriage work, I presented their choices to them: (1) keep everything just as it was; (2) make a radical shift, such as leaving the corporation, selling the house and moving to a smaller, slower-paced city where Jay could obtain less demanding, albeit less well compensated, employment; or (3) try to negotiate a 10% change. I developed this strategy in concert with my consultation group. The team predicted that Jay and Frieda would first reject these three options and choose a utopian solution for their problem, and that only after exploring the possibilities of such a solution would they recognize their inability to implement it.

True to the team's prediction, Frieda's and Jay's first reaction was that only a really *major* change in the relationship would be satisfactory but that this major change ought not to involve any threat to Jay's career, their social status, or their life-style. After two sessions of trying to envision major changes within their guidelines, a frustrated Jay and Frieda were forced to admit that they had created an impossible task for themselves. Eventually they agreed that the 10% change looked the most plausible, even if it did not seem nearly enough.

Many sessions were spent defining what a 10% change would be in various specific areas of the marriage. Each spouse would suggest what the other should do. I would then make the task and goal mutual, pointing out how, for instance, Frieda's efficiency in making social plans for the couple helped keep Jay incompetent in that role. The assignment would then be given for each spouse to do something different with respect to the issue they were working on. Frequently, after agreeing to do something different, Jay and Frieda reported failure. These "failed experiments" were the grist for many sessions of therapy, as both spouses learned to confront how they themselves participated in maintaining the system as it was. The eventual effect of such conversations was to reduce the animosity and blaming quality of the couple's relationship.

The issue with the highest potential for storm was the distribution of power in the marriage, but since the emotional atmosphere between them had improved, I decided the timing was good. I suggested that the deadness in the relationship which they had described early in therapy had in part been caused by the bystander quality of Frieda's involvement in all decisions of major importance. Although I was bringing up a subject they had not raised, I knew I was on the right track when Frieda began to act more lively and speak with more expression. Jay paled.

As Jay and Frieda recounted their usual way of thinking about decision-making, I gave them my impression that they had a stockholder's version: whoever has the most stock has the most votes, and number of stocks in their case (as in most cases) was being measured by salary. Both Jay and Frieda had been thinking this way. I challenged them to make a good case that Jay had more stock in the marriage than Frieda—more stake, that is, and more well-being riding on its success. They were actually pleased *not* to be able to say one had more stake than the other and it began to make sense to them that equal stake should mean consensual decision-making. They were confounded, however, as to what such a model might mean for them. I agreed with them about the difficulty it posed and offered no hope for easy solution. Instead, I suggested that this dilemma could serve as a barometer: the more they found it to be at the forefront, the more they could know that their commitment to improving the relationship was being honored by both of them.

After several more months, Jay and Frieda terminated therapy. They spent the last few sessions summarizing what had taken place in my office. No radical changes had been made in their lives, yet they both agreed that they felt greater respect for their own and each other's contribution to the marriage. They felt less need to blame the other for having "caused" the unhappiness and unfulfillment experienced in the marriage. Freed from the burden of that blame, the marriage had become a more tolerable and comfortable arrangement for Frieda and Jay.

Pitfalls

Working with couples in a corporate marriage holds several particular risks for the feminist family therapist. These risks are briefly explained below.

(1) *Shaking the tambourine.* If the therapist expresses too much zeal and anger at the inequities of the social order, she may preempt the clients' own expressions of those feelings, or prompt them to blame themselves for having been so stupid as to go along with the order of corporate life for all these years. Timing, guidance, the ability to modulate intensity, and a willingness to foster the clients' newly emerging way of seeing are critical skills for the therapist to use in handling her zeal.

(2) *Thinking Cinderella stories are just for other people.* The therapist's professional status may not fully protect her against cultural myths. The unwary therapist may find herself tripped up by unexpected envy of her woman client's economic situation. This envy may lead the therapist to discount the woman's problems or to overvalue the advantages of her situation.

(3) *Searching for the villain of the piece.* If the therapist chooses the corporation as the villain, what can she do about it? If she chooses society, how can she motivate her clients to do anything for themselves? If she chooses the husband, how will she keep him in therapy? If she chooses the wife, she is too late. The woman already did that.

(4) *Assuming we're all friends.* Kept women, unused to expressing hostility directly or admitting its presence, may give it to the therapist in covert ways, such as engaging only superficially in the therapy or disguising criticism of the therapist as friendly advice or innocent comments. The source of this hostility is that the therapist represents a threat to the client, a road not taken, proof that there *was* a choice to be made about how to live her own life. The therapist may not expect this hostility because she is used to being gratefully accepted by, understanding, and validating women. Caught unprepared, the therapist may interpret the client's hostility literally, instead of viewing it as a projection; or she may ignore it altogether, thereby allowing it to continue.

V

THE SINGLE PARENT FAMILY

*In the beginning was the Mother; the
Word began a later age, one we have
come to call patriarchy. . . . The
single universal covering . . . all
mammals and much other animal life
as well, is that the core of society, the
center of whatever kind of social
group exists, is mother and child.*

— *Marilyn French*, Beyond Power

PAULINE STOPPED ME in the hall one day and asked if we could talk for a moment. She is a computer programmer at the university, but since her department is several floors from mine, I do not see her often. The expression on her face let me know that a social visit was not on her mind, so I invited her down to my office.

Pauline told me she was having trouble with her thirteen year old son Billy. He was attending the fifth grade for the third time. Mary, 10, was repeating the fourth grade, but her grades were good. Tommy, 8, and Susie, 6, were doing fairly well in their school work. Pauline described Billy as a better student than Mary, and also said that he was a generous and thoughtful boy. "I depend on Billy for help with the other three, and for company," she said.

Although Billy had been tested as above average in intelligence, he was in the process of failing again. "He has a wonderful teacher this time, a black man who believes in giving extra help to black boys, but still Billy isn't passing. Maybe it's because his father has cut off contact with him, but that was two years ago." I could not get any clues from Pauline as to why she was so disturbed about

Billy's school work at the present time, since his school performance was obviously a chronic problem, or why Mary was not also a focus of concern. What came across most clearly was that Pauline was very eager to talk to someone. She said she thought it was time for professional help.

The description Pauline had given about Billy's teacher led me to believe that she held race to be a significant dimension in a helping relationship. Consequently, I told Pauline that I knew a black therapist who was quite experienced with young teens and their families, and offered to refer her. Without hesitation she declined, saying that she preferred to work with me, and that Billy would accept that decision. We made an appointment for later that week and I invited her to bring the whole family.

We have here the typical broken home: beleaguered mother, uncontrolled kids, and no man to keep things in line. No, we have here the typical black matriarchal household: over-controlling mother, kids straining at the bit, and no man able to be as good as she is. No, we have here the typical modern woman: Supermom, kids who are expected to prove her excellence, and no man necessary, thank you.

These negative stereotypes are present for both the therapist and the family, and affect their impressions of themselves and of one another. Peggy Papp has described the "problem-generating cycle" potentially involved in such interactions (1984, p. xvi). Single mothers, convinced by popular opinion that they are inadequate, begin to view their children as problematic and seek out experts to help them. Therapists accept such families for treatment uncritically, thus confirming the mothers' original fears.

We believe that the negative views and assumptions about the single-parent family are really about the single-mother family. Over 90% of children in single-parent families live with their mother (Masnick and Bane, 1980). Those who live with their single father meet a very different situation. First, there is the matter of money: he is almost certain to have more. Second, there is the matter of social opinion: his home does not look so deprived to the outside viewer and he can hire someone to perform what are seen as motherly duties, or his own mother or sister may step in. The single mother is unlikely in these ways to obtain a substitute father. Social opinion builds its negative case on this shortage. Third, the single father is seen as a hero, a sympathetic figure who is admired and congratulated for his willingness and capacity to do it all. The single mother is seen as a failure, a suspicious figure who is sometimes pitied but more often criticized for getting herself in this position.

The stereotypes and negative images that therapist and family must address together have to do with women, and the single-*mother* family is the focus of this chapter.

Pauline and Her Children

I spent a good part of the first session getting to know each of the children. They were very polite and reasonably attentive, but predictably uninformative about why they had been brought to therapy. I sensed that this was a close family, and noticed that Pauline and her children spoke to each other respectfully and with obvious affection. I asked a few questions about everyday family life, but at every chance Pauline brought the focus of the conversation back to Billy.

We spent the remainder of the first session specifically talking about Billy's school problem. Pauline's concern was that he might be retained again in the fifth grade. The worst of it was, she said, that Billy was a bright boy, and could certainly do the work if he put his mind to it. She could not understand why he would not try. Billy had no explanation either. Sometimes he "just forgot" his homework, or "just didn't finish" his classroom assignments. Since I wanted to be responsive to the symptom they presented, I offered to call the school and speak with Billy's teacher. Pauline was transparently delighted at this suggestion. I asked Billy for his opinion. He said, "That will be okay; my teacher won't lie."

Billy's teacher said he was as confused about Billy as everyone else. "He's a bright kid," the teacher said, "I think he has some leadership potential. The work is not too difficult for him. He has no social problems. I have no idea, really." The teacher reported that Billy gave all the right answers to the counselors, principal, and school psychologist about what it takes to be successful, but that in practice, he did completely the opposite. The teacher had spent considerable extra effort on Billy, consulting with Pauline about homework being assigned to Billy, and offering to call her whenever Billy failed to turn in an assignment. As a result, homework was not as serious a problem as it had been (although Billy would occasionally fail to turn in an assignment his mother had watched him complete), but Billy frequently turned in classroom assignments of blank pages.

When I asked when the problem began, Pauline talked about Billy's father. Frank was Pauline's first adult relationship. They were very close for a couple of years, but never married. Frank never supported Billy financially, although he occasionally sent gifts. In the summer of 1984, Billy went to visit his father for a week and got caught in the middle of a fight between Frank and his wife. The wife left town in a fury, and Frank followed her after leaving Billy with his grandmother, telling the boy that he would be back in a day or two. A week later Pauline went to pick up Billy; Frank never called. Later they learned that Frank had moved and acquired an unlisted phone number. Billy had not heard from his father since then. According to Pauline, it was around this time that Billy's school problems began.

During that same summer Pauline left Harry her husband and the father of the three younger children. Pauline had married him in 1975. Their relationship was a stormy one, punctuated by a couple of long separations. Three months after their most recent reconciliation, Pauline discovered that Harry had fathered a child by a woman he had been seeing for several years. That, in addition to the fact that he was not offering the family financial support and was "drinking a lot" motivated Pauline to leave him. The three younger children were upset by the separation, but Pauline reported that Billy had never liked Harry, and was relieved that his mother finally left him. Still, Pauline had not filed for a divorce. "My mother, my church, and my own self are against divorce," she said.

In the following session I asked questions about the family's life together. Pauline was attending school at night three evenings each week, in addition to working at a full-time job. When she was away, Billy was in charge of the other three children, but all of them agreed that basically they each took care of themselves. Over all, Pauline had no complaints about the children's behavior at home. She said she was also proud of their behavior at church where they, along with Pauline, took leadership roles. My impression was that she adored her children and that they responded in kind.

Billy's special role in the family seemed to be that of being his mother's companion. On the three nights of the week that she was at school, he would wait up for her, and when she got home they would talk and sometimes play checkers. Whenever she was late coming home, he worried that she had been mugged, and on rainy nights he feared for her safety driving on the slippery streets.

All of the information I was getting in therapy was coming to me in threads that I was having trouble weaving together. There seemed to be many possibilities about the purpose of Billy's symptom, but I found it hard to verify any of them. I decided to try a behavioral intervention that I thought might work regardless of the purpose or etiology of Billy's symptom. I wanted to address Billy's presented problem directly while at the same time de-focusing the problem from him.

I met with the children as a group and set up a reward plan for doing good schoolwork. Each of the children earned points toward a reward (a quarter or a soft drink) by doing satisfactory homework. The plan worked for a while, but became easily complicated by assignments that did not fit the parameters or by teachers who forgot to sign the work. We would then renegotiate, a process the children enjoyed, but each version would only work for a week or two before getting hopelessly complicated again. The other problem with the intervention was that it did not seem to make much difference in how Billy performed his classroom work, or in anyone's mood about the problem.

I then asked to see both Pauline and Billy individually. Throughout our family sessions, Pauline had appeared to like talking to me and had said a number of things that made me think she highly identified with me as a single mother and professional woman. Yet any time it seemed that we were about to work on an issue other than Billy, such as her marriage, or her plans for her own life, the conversation always sputtered out and died. Our individual session was no different. I was not used to having such difficulty homing in on a workable problem in therapy. I wondered if Pauline belonged in the category of the "worried well," someone who comes to see the doctor with a touch of something, having heard of awful things going around and wanting to keep healthy. Still, Billy *was* failing the fifth grade for the *third* time.

In my session with Billy, I asked him to be the counselor and advise me on how to handle a kid having trouble turning in his work. I wanted to check out the possibility that Billy's poor school performance might be connected to a desire to get his father to return to the family.

Billy: It's probably a family problem, a discipline problem, or a mental problem.

T: What kind of family problem could it be?

B: Money, divorce, fear for mom, death.

T: What would you advise if it is a family problem?

B: Send the kid and his family to a counselor.

T: Okay, you be the counselor. My family problem is that my dad has left my mom and I'm doing bad in school. If I do bad enough, maybe my dad will come back.

B: That won't happen.

T: Well, what can I do to bring him back?

B: You'd better leave that alone, that's between your mother and your father. It's their business.

T: But he has left me too. He never calls me or comes to see me. Could I have done something?

B: No. It sounds like your father has a problem. Talk to him.

T: He won't talk to me.

B: Then you'll just have to be sad.

T: Will I keep failing in school because I'm so sad?

B: No, (laughing as though that's a ridiculous idea), you have to use good workmanship even though you are sad.

As we ended the roleplay, Billy volunteered, "You know, they don't make kids repeat the fifth grade more than twice. I'll be promoted to sixth grade next year no matter what." "So," I said, "you don't intend to try to pass, do you?" "No," he said, having the last laugh.

That did it. Every trail I had been down thus far had led to a dead end. Billy's reason for failing the fifth grade again was now clear and reasonable. It left me without a clear goal for the therapy. I had no idea what to do next. I took my quandary to the consulting group.

Consultation

The therapist said that trying to find a workable problem with Pauline was like trying to catch a tadpole in a densely populated pond. The consulting group acknowledged her frustration in attempting a problem-focused therapy that seemed to get away as soon as she got closer. All of us wondered with her what was making the course of therapy so slippery. We began to explore the context of the family's life, reviewing the difficulties that single mothers face. Their time and energy is more stretched than that of any other working parent. They are more prone to guilt regarding their children than other working mothers because sole parental responsibility is so obviously and publicly on their shoulders. Compared to married people, they generally need and expect more from their children, and are less supported in their own personal needs. In this particular case we acknowledged that as four white therapists discussing the life of a black single working mother, there was an entire set of experiences in Pauline's life different from our own. We decided to stay alert to the possibility that this might affect the therapy, the problem, or the relationship with the therapist, but not to prejudge that effect.

Then we turned our attention to the presented problem: Billy's school performance. What did we think was wrong with him that caused him to fail the fifth grade twice, with a good possibility that he might fail again? We came up with several hypotheses that traditional family therapy might suggest:

First, Billy might be designated a "parentified" child. Was he overburdened with chores for a child of thirteen? Was he inappropriately used as a confidant, given information that could only confuse him? The therapist informed us about the tasks in the home and the content of the talks between Pauline and Billy, none of which struck us as onerous. We decided that in this case those conditions were not injurious, and that Billy's poor school performance was not a child's cry for help about an excessive load. We also noted that if we used as the standard the *idealized* image of two-parent families, Billy did seem to work harder and have more responsibility.

Second, it might be suggested that Billy felt deserted by his biological father and most recently by his stepfather, and then became either too sad, too angry, or too hopeless to bother with school. This hypothesis is a frequent one in circumstances like Billy's and is based on the assumed importance of the presence of the father in a child's life. In holding that assumption to be generally true, family therapy confuses an idealization of the family with the reality of family. Fathers are less involved than many theoretical descriptions would suggest. While it may be an excellent goal of family therapy to have fathers more involved, the absence of fathers through separation or divorce does not in itself *necessarily* lead to negative repercussions for children. In any case, Billy showed no evidence of sadness, anger, or hopelessness.

A third common hypothesis would be that Billy was worried about his mother and believed that he needed to stay around longer and not advance to the next grade in order to take care of her. This hypothesis ignores the fact that the majority of black children—with the exception of those upper income black families that emulate the gender role behavior of white families—have a different picture of womanhood than the one constructed by white society. In general, the black child's experience of woman is that she is strong—soft, nurturing, and strong. Although Billy might be afraid on a rainy night that his mother would have an accident, that fear is different from being afraid that she is not competent enough to manage what he is too young to be able to manage. In contrast, white children, particularly boys, would be more inclined to believe by Billy's age that women are weak and need protection by a man, regardless of his age. This has not been Billy's experience.

Fourth, it could be suggested that Billy took on the job of distracting his mother from her depression after the marital separation by keeping her concerned and busy with him. This assumption is based on the idea, widely held by strategic/systemic therapists, that children sense their parents' upset and figure out ways to distract them from their sadness, a kind of "collusive mischief" (Hoffmann, 1981, p. 84). Although this concept may be applicable in many cases where parents have separated, there was no evidence that Pauline was depressed. Furthermore, Pauline had been managing the household successfully for two years without any emotional or financial assistance from the children's fathers.

After rejecting these four hypotheses, we arrived at our final working perspective: Billy's problems with school began around the time when Billy's father and stepfather withdrew. Perhaps Billy was upset and dispirited and as his school work started to decline, his mother stepped in to help him along. Since the origins were lost to us, we could not know for certain. What we were surer of was that at the time of therapy, Billy was not upset and did have the ability to do his work. Whatever circumstance initially established Pauline's involvement with Billy's work, the involvement now was being maintained out of Billy's desire for his mother's special attention and Pauline's desire for Billy to pass. We are not suggesting that Billy was failing in order to keep his mother close. Rather, we observed that both Billy and Pauline enjoyed the interactions and wanted them both to recognize that it could be useful and pleasurable for Pauline to experience Billy as smart and for Billy to show her his intelligence. However, what stood out for us was that, as Billy said, he would be promoted anyway.

We agreed that Billy had a point. There was no need for him to improve his work since his promotion at this point was guaranteed. His pride steered him away from trying. Not trying put distance between him and this otherwise degrading circumstance. Pauline and Billy could work together because it was an enjoyable activity, not because they feared his failure. We surmised that Pauline had called a family therapist in the hope of figuring out what was wrong with Billy, and in so doing underestimated the effect on Billy of the school's decision to promote him, underestimated Billy (that he understood the situation and decided not to try), and underestimated herself (that she was doing a fine job).

According to some reports, black families typically seek psychotherapy over their concern about how poor school adjustment might affect future employment and are most responsive to family therapy focused on the child (Hines and Boyd-Franklin, 1982). Pauline seemed to fit that description so far. We agreed with the therapist that she should continue to engage Pauline in her concern about Billy, judging it likely that removing the focus from Billy might lead to losing Pauline as a client. We also believed it important to avoid letting the content about Billy blot out a perspective on what Pauline herself needed. Pauline had been offered the opportunity to be referred to a black therapist, but she had declined, stating her preference to work with our colleague. In our view, this decision reflected Pauline's desire for affirmation from a woman who was not only familiar to her but was a single working mother also, and could affirm that her children were good and loving and that she was a competent woman and mother. We suggested that the therapist be an affirming colleague to Pauline who was exploring how she felt about her roles as mother, worker, and wife.

Analysis

Statistics reported for 1985 show that there are nearly four million white single-mother households and nearly two million black single-mother households (United States Department of Commerce National Data Book and Guide to Sources, 1987). A better comparison by race is to say that the proportion of black households that are single mother families is four times the proportion for whites (United States Department of Commerce National Data Book and Guide to Sources, 1987). By 1990 one-half of all our children under 18 will spend 3–5 years living in a single-mother family (Glick, 1979). Despite the fact that this family model is widespread, stigma for being a member of it nevertheless persists and acts as an etiologic factor in many of its problems.

The stigma involves an assumption of detrimental effects on the family members, the "victims" of divorce: the children will not be properly disciplined, will suffer problems of sexual identity and confusion about gender role; they will be troubled and will get into trouble. The mother will be lonely, inept, and sexually hungry; she will prey upon the husbands of friends and neighbors. Through neglect and distraction, she will invite misfortunes to befall her children.

What accounts for such a jaundiced view, one that ignores possible strength and assumes only deficiency? In large part, it is because the culture has a near-sighted focus on the absence of a significant man to give legitimate status and safe harbor. "Broken," the term frequently used to refer to mother/children families, reflects that focus and signals an inferior and deviant arrangement. Note that the term is rarely used to refer to the widow-headed family, a more socially acceptable and sympathetic arrangement, with the husband absent through no presumed fault of the wife.

The stigma for the single mother derives from more than just the absence of a man. As one report put it: "The deviance is twofold—not only is there one adult rather than two in the family constellation, but the family head is female rather than male. Not only is the type of family deviant, but the mother herself is assuming a deviant gender role" (Brandwein, Brown, and Fox, 1974, p. 498). Society is loath to recognize and accept a woman in the independent, responsible position "normally" reserved for a man. If our culture were a matriarchy instead of a patriarchy, the mother-headed/father-absent model would look less stunted, less damaged, and less embarrassing.

This prejudice creates hardships. On a broad scale, it is reflected in the failure to establish subsidized social supports such as daycare and housekeeping. On a personal scale, the single mother typically takes on a general expectation of inferior performance, despite the fact that she generally would have major responsibility for care of the house and children in any case. Pauline expressed a sense of insecurity and shame because of this. The prejudice also affects interpersonal interaction. A single mother often faces exploitative attitudes and actions by various men from neighbors who trespass on her property to bankers who treat her with disrespect — all because she "does not belong to anyone."

There is also the matter of money. Economic discrimination against women in the job market combines with financial abandonment by fathers to force single mothers and their children into severe difficulties. Only one-third of single mothers receive child support, and two-thirds of the payments are less than the court-ordered amount (Hacker, 1982). As a result, 42.7% of white children and 65.6% of black children who live with their single mothers live in poverty (U. S. Census, 1978).

Given the stigma and the hardships, it would not be surprising to discover dismal outcomes for such mothers and children, both as individuals and as families. Much evidence however is in the opposite direction. Research indicates that the majority of single-mother families are as successful on various measures as two-parent families, when compared at similar levels of income. On measures of emotional adjustment, IQ, scholastic achievement, and culturally expected "masculine" behavior in boys, children fare equally well in both kinds of families. Except for the greater likelihood of poverty for children with single mothers, there are only two differences noted between the groups. One is that girls from single-mother households are more independent and more competent than girls from households with a father present. Second, some children from single-mother families show lower self-esteem, but researchers report that the cause is prejudiced social opinion, not family structure. (These findings are summarized and documented in Cashion's review of major studies [1982]).

Research also describes other aspects of living in this family model. Warmth and closeness are characteristic, created by and reflected in the participation of all family members in tasks, decision-making, and rewards (Weiss, 1979). In contrast to the two-parent family where mother and father establish a hierarchy with themselves at the top (father a bit more at the top than mother) and the children at the bottom, the single-mother family typically functions as a consensual arrangement. Generally there is little conflict and the single mother feels better able to manage routines and resources, even when scarce, because the consultative process with her children gives her a greater sense of power and competence than she would have as the wife of someone who not only dominates the children but her as well (Brandwein et al., 1979; Cashion, 1982). As for the children, their greater responsibility in these households is rewarded by greater power, for example more participation in deciding where the family goes for fun, how tasks can be divided, and what schedule suits their needs.

These findings suggest some alternative assumptions that should be made about important elements of family structure and function:

A family does not need two parents to make it a family. Mother and children can carry out the economic, domestic, social, and psychological functions that define family. In this regard, we differ with Morawetz and Walker (1984) who suggest single-parent "household" as a more accurate term than single-parent family. In our view, such usage continues to deny family status to the mother/children grouping. To the extent that the non-custodial father takes an active part in the life of his children when they are with him, we would prefer to say that mother/children are a single-parent family, and that the children are members of another single-parent family when with their father.

A family does not need a hierarchical structure to make it work. Our criticism of family therapy theory is its failure to apply what has been found true for the single-parent family to family in general. Instead, it has continued to promote hierarchy as the primary organizing principle of family. To hold to hierarchy as the best way to accomplish the functions of family validates the idea that power is the highest good, hierarchy is the best way to embody it, and domination is the best way to exercise it.

If mother and children can work well as a democracy, why can the same not be true of mother, father and children? Why the continued, unchallenged teaching about "protecting" the parental dyad by a firm boundary to mark a clear hierarchy, as if that arrangement were in the best interest of *all* the members? Yet when Father is no longer a part of the household, so the teaching goes, hierarchy is no longer necessary (Fulmer, 1983; Minuchin, 1974). How is it that the correlation between Father and hierarchy goes unmentioned?

Because of its unexamined commitment to patriarchy, family therapy remains committed to hierarchy. The "king of his castle" ideology, and not family health, gives hierarchy its grip on theory. What tightens the grip is a keystone of men's psychology described by Jean Baker Miller: " . . . in the family setting, men very early in life acquire the sense that they are members of a superior group. Things are supposed to be done for them by those lesser people who work at trying to do so. From then on, cooperativeness may appear to men as if it were somehow detracting from themselves" (1976, p. 42). By contrast, women do not experience cooperation as loss, but rather as gain, as enlargement.

What would cooperative democracy in family life mean? It would mean that the goal was to meet the needs of each member of the family, but that the gains of one member were not to be won at the expense of another. It would mean that parents would provide children with guidelines for health, safety, and morality, and with necessities they could not supply for themselves, but that in the unnumbered daily ways where preference rather than well-being was at issue, there would be room for difference, individual action, and experimental solutions. It would mean that those with superior resources and knowledge would use that power to strengthen other members of the family, not to control them and garner more power for themselves. It would mean that parents would demonstrate to children how to compromise and negotiate and how to avoid power struggles rather than how to set them up (Pogrebin, 1983).

The Single Black Mother

Now that a substantial number of white women are working outside the home and caring for their children on their own, the country is beginning to pay attention to the single working mother's experience. Still, however, there is insufficient social commitment to make a significant difference regarding work hours, child care, and pay scales. When this circumstance was primarily the black woman's experience there was little attention paid to her burden, or her resourcefulness; any interest was almost exclusively concern about her children.

Society had an interest in the children, for it was the children of the black single working mothers that many social scientists believed were doomed for poverty and crime. The mothers were worthy of national attention only in reference to the children: Why are there so many single black mothers? How can society dissuade more black women from becoming single parents? What is it about these women and these men that they are unable to maintain a healthy two-parent family system? Is the single black mother responsible for the dysfunction of her children? Is the breakdown of the black family the cause of the economic and social weakness of black Americans?

This last question was answered in the affirmative in the controversial Moynihan Report which began with the assertion that "at the heart of the deterioration of the fabric of Negro society is the deterioration of the Negro family" (Moynihan, 1965/1971, p. 126). Moynihan blames the "breakdown" of the black family for black poverty, illegitimacy, poor school performance, delinquency, and crime. He asserts that the root of the problem was slavery, which vitiated family life, creating a fatherless matrifocal family structure. The subsequent power of the mother and the powerlessness (read: absence) of the father have created the contemporary problems among blacks, according to Moynihan. His message is quite clear: beware of female headed households — they can ruin an entire race.

From a feminist point of view, this argument is absurd and wrong. Even the history is incorrect. Particularly noteworthy here is the description Genovese gives of the black family under slavery: "What has usually been viewed as a debilitating female supremacy was in fact a closer approximation to a healthy sexual equality than was possible for whites and perhaps even for postbellum blacks" (1974, p. 500).

The Moynihan Report has been discredited by numerous scholars. We address it however because its thesis has become part of popular culture. Therapists who work with black mothers need to be conscious of its influence on them and their clients.

Besides divorce, illegitimacy, and desertion, Moynihan views the fact of women as head of family as another indicator of family pathology. Further, he believes that in two-parent black families where the mother works, the family's dependence on the mother's income "undermines the position of the father and deprives the children of the kind of attention, particularly in school matters, which is now a standard feature of middle-class upbringing" (1965/1971, p. 138). Pauline, who shares in this culture's middle class values, must certainly have absorbed this denunciation of her efforts.

Virtually all Moynihan's assertions are based on his assumption that the white middle class family structure (father as head of the family, a mother who stays at home) is responsible for the success of white children and that the inverse structure is responsible for the failure of black children. Moynihan writes:

Ours is a society which presumes male leadership in private and public affairs. The arrangements of society facilitate such leadership and reward it. A subculture, such as that of the Negro American, in which this is not the pattern is placed at a distinct disadvantage (1965/1971, p. 140).

Although Moynihan admits that the problems for Blacks in America are complex, he nevertheless asserts that the "weakness of the family structure" is at the "center of the tangle of pathology" (1965/1971, p. 142). Moynihan illustrates this weakness by pointing to the frequent role reversal of wife and husband, the superior education of black women compared to black men, the absence of the father as head of household, and the matriarchal pattern that predominates in black families. His solution to the problems faced by the black American is to strengthen the family—to establish a family structure that parallels the white middle-class, hierarchical, and father-ruled American family of the 1950s.

It is over twenty years now since the Moynihan Report was issued. Many of his findings have been refuted and his basic assumptions challenged. The white middle-class American family that he used as his benchmark has itself changed. Today, it is the changing white family that has much to learn from the black family for its variability, diversity, and resourcefulness, and from the example set by the single black working mother for her strength and courage. We are reminded of what Angela Davis wrote about black women under slavery:

> It was those women who passed on to their nominally free female descendants a legacy of hard work, perseverance and self-reliance, a legacy of tenacity, resistance and insistence on sexual equality—in short a legacy spelling out standards for a new womanhood (1981, p. 29).

Treatment

Goals

Our goals with Pauline and her family were:

(1) To underscore Pauline's competence as a mother.
(2) To defocus Pauline from her concern with Billy's performance at school and help her shift to a more positive view of Billy as a student while continuing her positive view of the other children as students.

(3) To help Pauline and her children affirm their particular family as well-functioning and rid themselves of negative connotations associated with its being a single-mother family.

(4) To listen carefully to Pauline for signs that she was not hearing her own voice, that she was acting, thinking, or feeling as others would wish or expect her to, rather than on her own behalf.

Plan

Competence. Pauline did many things well that she did not give herself credit for: her children were basically happy and well-behaved; she was financially independent; she was a pillar of her church; and she was actively involved in improving her life by pursuing her education. Yet she found it easy to doubt herself and to see her faults rather than her skills. The therapist could demonstrate her trust of Pauline's competence by not rushing in to give advice, by encouraging Pauline to explore her own solutions, and by making sure Pauline gave herself credit for her successes. Pauline could be helped to affirm Billy's competence once her negative interpretation of his school performance had been removed.

Defocusing. Pauline was concerned that her involvement with Billy over his homework had no discernible effect on his in-school behavior. The therapist could work along two fronts to change Pauline's view about that. First, she can point out the irrelevance of Billy's school performance since it was disconnected to his promotion, while reminding Pauline that Billy was very aware of this. Second, she could take every opportunity with Pauline to underscore how well Billy was doing in other aspects of his life, as a brother, son, and friend.

Affirmation. Pauline had expectations regarding the consequences of being a single mother which lead her to question her own abilities and the well-being of her children. Significantly, she chose a therapist who was also a single mother and whom Pauline identified as competent at that task. The therapist could use this to support Pauline by drawing parallels between their experiences.

She could use self-disclosure to point out similar dilemmas she faces as a single parent and to affirm for Pauline that occasional problem raising children is a normal event in the lives of all parents. The therapist could also help Pauline identify biases from friends, church, extended family members, and society in general that define the single-mother family as deviant and inferior.

Listening. Pauline had listened attentively to the teachings of her family, her church, and her culture. She wanted to do what was right, wanted people to think well of her. She was less successful listening to her own voice, making decisions on the basis of what *she* wanted and what would be best for *her*. This issue came up most clearly when she mentioned divorce. Pauline's reasons for staying married to Harry had to do with meeting the expectations of others, rather than reflecting her own needs and desires. The therapist must listen for signs of what Pauline wants, what Pauline thinks would be best for her. As Pauline is not adept at hearing her own voice, the therapist must act as an amplifier for her, picking up and enlarging each statement which contains information about Pauline's own point of view.

Pauline and Her Children

As the school year came to a close, there was no sustained improvement in Billy's school performance though he continued to perform well on schoolwork with his mother. Once Pauline realized Billy would actually move on to the next grade, I helped her let go of the hope of his getting better grades and instead take pride in the knowledge and skill he exhibited with her. True to his prediction, he was placed in the sixth grade for the following year. After school was out, the level of tension in the household subsided. All four children became involved in activities organized by the neighborhood and the church, and I took many opportunities to comment to Pauline on their abilities to manage themselves, engage with others, act as leaders, and carry responsibility.

Pauline brought in few complaints about the children. Once she reported that Billy had broken a neighbor child's bicycle, after Pauline had specifically told him to stay off of it because it was too small for him. "I had to ground him," she told me tearfully. "I can't understand why he does bad things like that." Although I offered her reassurance, I thought she was more upset than was warranted by the circumstance. I could not find anything else that was going on which would explain her reaction. I thought that she must be very unsure about her competence to react so strongly to such normal childish misbehavior. Given how critically the culture looks at single mothers—especially black single mothers—this made sense to me. I did nothing more with this incident other than support her regarding the appropriateness of her discipline and the difficulty of understanding one's children. The issue never came up again, but occasionally Pauline would report to me other examples of the children's misbehavior and her responses. In every case it seemed that she just needed to recount for my ears how she handled discipline. Once I affirmed that she seemed to have handled it well, she would be visibly relieved.

As worries over the children lessened and Pauline seemed more at ease with me, I made some attempts to gauge her interest in talking about herself. She did offer more than she had earlier, but she had an internal alarm which rang whenever she felt she had spent too much of a session talking about herself. After just a few minutes of such exploration, she would automatically switch to talking about Billy. Sometimes I would say, "Wait. I'm not through with you yet," and she would smile, pleased to be regarded as important in her own right, and would begin on her own issues again. However, I remembered my discussion with the consulting team and did not want to push too hard for a focus on herself.

Piecemeal, she gave me her own history. She was the oldest of three daughters raised by a mother who worked two jobs to support her family after her husband left for another woman, when Pauline was eight. After Pauline and her sisters were grown their mother remarried a man twenty years her senior. "The biggest attraction was that he told her she'd never have to work again." According to Pauline, it remains an awful marriage, and her mother "lives like a prisoner. She drinks a lot now." Pauline is determined not to end up like her mother, but sees parallels that scare her. "We're both hard workers, and both our husbands chased around on us. Neither one of us believes in divorce."

Talking about her mother seemed to ease the way for Pauline to begin to address her relationship with Harry. Since she had been so reluctant to approach the topic at all, I realized it was essential that she not see me as advocating a position for her. My task was to keep the conversation going, to let her voice her intense ambivalence regarding divorce. Any statement about Harry's self-destructive behaviors would be followed by an evaluative comment like "divorce equals failure to me. It means I've failed in what I meant to do, failed in my commitment to keep with the marriage no matter what. It's wrong to get divorced. My church doesn't believe in it and I don't either."

It seemed to me that Pauline was approaching divorce by searching for legitimate reasons, by saying them aloud and seeing how they sounded both to her and to me. I facilitated this process by asking for evaluations of various aspects of the situation: What are the children thinking about the situation lately? What kind of person does Harry seem to be these days? How would your life be different if he came back? Nothing Pauline ever said suggested Harry had changed in a way that might make the marriage more tolerable for her. She was full of contradictions. Her assessment of the single mothers she knew was that "they seem happier, more in control than married mothers. They don't have to ask permission. They come home and say to the kids: 'Let's go,' and they all go without having to ask Dad if that's okay." Yet she also felt that she was denying her children some irreplaceable benefit by divorcing this man though he had not contributed to their financial or emotional well-being in over two years. She feared the racist attitudes that would cause her children to be harshly judged as the children of a single black mother. Having had my opportunity to speak my own opinion to my consulting group made it considerably easier for me to remain in a neutral position with respect to Pauline's decision regarding divorce.

Discussions about the advisability of divorce continued for four or five sessions spread over the summer. I noticed that each time Pauline shifted in her ambivalence, the children shifted also. When she was ready to take Harry back, so were they, and when she was leaning in the direction of proceeding with a divorce, they said that this was probably the best solution. I understood their agreement as demonstrating the reality of how the children viewed Harry in their life: "If Mother wants him, fine; otherwise, we can do without him."

One day Pauline excitedly called me up to say that Harry wanted to come in for a session. She sounded as if she thought this was a very big breakthrough. When I asked her what led up to his request, she said that Billy told Harry what he said in a session about Harry not being a good father; now Harry wanted to set a few things straight with me. I told Pauline that I would be happy to meet with Harry, but I needed to have some idea of our agenda. Did Harry want to discuss his relationship with Billy? Was he interested in discussing the future of his relationship with Pauline? I asked Pauline to find out. In our next session Pauline reported that Harry said he was not interested in working on *any* relationship, but that he just wanted to tell me not to believe everything that Billy said. Pauline was both sad and indignant about this lost opportunity. What looked like Harry's interest in the family had given her hope that a reconciliation might follow. Finding out she was wrong became the stimulus for her to begin giving up hope that the marriage might have a future. She began to describe herself as "finished" with Harry, a position which the children immediately endorsed. Billy, who had been the most vocal of the children in his disapproval of Harry, was obviously relieved. Pauline confided to me that Billy had warned her that Harry would "pull her down" if she went back to him.

After the session in which she announced that she was "finished" with Harry, Pauline started thinking about herself for the first time as a single mother. She said:

> I respect you so much. You have made it in a man's world and you have children you are raising alone, and you're always so cordial and I just admire you so. I want to make it too, but I was always told when I was a girl that all I could be is a maid. I'm trying so hard to be something else, and I'm trying so hard with my family. I don't know what is happening to our black families. It's like a plague has hit them: the men are gone and have nothing to do with their children and they don't support us financially. I guess there's no need for me to be afraid; I've made it alone for two years.

I told Pauline that although I obviously could not speak first hand, my studies had taught me how hard this country has always made it for the black family to stay together. I could speak first hand as a single mother and I did. I told her I also get afraid: Will there be enough money? Is there someone I am neglecting? When is there time for me? We talked about not letting our fear stop us and observed that so far, both our experiences belied the prejudices that undermined our confidence.

Just before the new school year began, we had another family session. The family discussed how the school year schedule was going to be arranged. Pauline had decided to rearrange her own school schedule from weeknights to Saturdays. On two evenings during the week, she was going to be selling a line of health foods. She said she felt encouraged and hopeful about the coming year. I asked the children to tell me how they thought their mother was doing. Billy took the floor and said with a proud smile that she was being strong with Harry. When I looked to Pauline for clarification, she told me that she had taken Harry to court for nonpayment of child support, and had his wages garnished. I knew that this was a major step for Pauline, and spoke to her about it in terms of its indication that she was doing a competent job of looking out for her children's interest.

For Pauline to make the decision to divorce Harry meant seeing her options as different from her mother's (who was still living within an abusive relationship), going against her church (which advised her to live a celibate life), and giving up her ambition of staying married in order not to end up another statistic about the failure of black families. I repeatedly pointed out how difficult it must be to resist all this pressure to comply with other people's expectations, and emphasized her independence as her strength.

Her decision to divorce Harry seemed to open up many sides of Pauline that had remained inaccessible or invisible to her as long as she was engaged in the dilemma about him. Throughout the fall we met in individual sessions, exploring her family relationships, professional directions, and personal history, all from the standpoint of where she had been and where she wanted to go, what she had had and what she wanted to have. In other words, she did not talk as if there were problems to solve, but rather mused on the possibilities within herself.

From time to time during these sessions, Pauline gave me news of the children. Billy was performing very well in sixth grade. She said she was also pleased to see that he had opened up more around the house. The other three children were doing well at school and were participating, as was Billy, in music and sports.

Pauline started dating several different men, breaking off with one of them after a few dates because "he believes women are below men. 'Do you like to cook?' he says. I like to cook fine, but I don't want to stand over a stove just to make him fat."

In our last session Pauline told me, "I'm proud of myself. I'm smarter now. I see that I ignored things about Harry that were signs that he was domineering and inconsiderate. I prefer to be by myself rather than be ordered around." Pauline left therapy believing in her own competence as a person and as a mother, feeling empowered to proceed with her life, pursuing her goals for herself and her family.

Pitfalls

These are the pitfalls that await the feminist family therapist working with a single-parent family:

(1) *Listening through rose-colored glasses.* The feminist family therapist so wants the single mother to emerge triumphant that she may actually minimize her client's problems. This danger is even more present with black clients because the picture of the strong black matriarch is so compelling and long-standing.

(2) *Chasing every ball.* The same impulse that would lead a feminist family therapist to minimize her client's particular problems may also lead her to maximize them. Eager to be helpful to a mother in an overwhelming situation, she may treat each mentioned problem as equally necessary to solve. Such a response implies not only that the mother is incompetent (and needs professional help to solve her every problem), but also that everything is top priority for immediate action. The mother's own reactions are thereby paralleled. The sense of being overwhelmed will increase for the mother, and the therapist will soon join her in it.

(3) *Passing on the torch.* Because the single-mother family is stigmatized and because the stigma is rooted in patriarchal views, the feminist family therapist will likely want her clients to see themselves as a *cause célèbre*, able to make noticeable inroads into prejudiced attitudes. The therapist will need to resist the impulse to lecture her clients on the errors inherent in the prejudice, looking instead for chances to show the family members how their own experience refutes the stereotype.

(4) *Getting ahead of the client.* The therapist's feminism sensitizes her to the problem of women staying in marriages that have ceased to exist for them in any meaningful way. In her eagerness to help the client get on with her life, the therapist may short-circuit the client's need to discover for herself that her marriage is past saving, and to then mourn its loss. The therapist who does not allow this process is replicating the client's familiar experience of not having her position respected.

VI
THE STANDARD PAIRING

Jack Sprat could eat no fat,
His wife could eat no lean,
And so between them both, you see,
They licked the platter clean.

— *Mother Goose*

HE IS UNEXCITABLE, methodical, most comfortable with literal facts, and obviously uncomfortable with emotion. She is excitable, unpredictable, most comfortable with feelings, and obviously uncomfortable with hard and fast rules. Many couples both in and out of therapy fit this description.

The concept of complementarity is often employed by family therapists to describe such couples and how their interaction leads to polarization. It is not simply that she is emotional, and he is rational; they seem to push each other to the extreme. Emotionality becomes hysteria; rationality becomes obsessiveness. Her capacity for intimacy becomes hostile dependency; his cool reserve becomes belligerent distancing.

Complementarity, however, focuses on interactions, not persons, and therefore directs us away from a glaring fact: it is always the men who show one set of characteristics, and the women who show the other. The characteristics are not randomly distributed; they are gender-determined. Indeed, these men and women compose such clearly delineated gender stereotypes as to seem a caricature of male/female coupling.

The merely cybernetic descriptions which dominate most family therapy literature approach marital interactions without the richness of content necessary for understanding the pairing under discussion. The descriptive term that comes to mind is "hystericobsessional relationship," borrowing from psychoanalytic theory. Psychoanalytic theory may indeed help to elaborate the description, but just like family therapy theories, it leaves out a key point. For that, we draw on feminism.

The feminist lens lets us see that we are not dealing with two sides of the same coin with these couples. Whereas society applauds the obsessive for his thoroughness, his attention to details, his obedience to the letter of the law, and his calm objectivity, it pathologizes the hysteric for her flightiness, her generalizations, her emotionalism, and her subjectivity. He, the good worker, makes up our work force. She, the good patient, makes up our caseload.

Gary and Jean

Gary and Jean, an attractive couple in their mid-forties, had been married two years when they came to me for marital therapy. Gary was a supervisor in an insurance company; Jean, a high school teacher in a private school. Jean presented herself to me as angry and unrelenting in her determination to see that her husband, Gary, either lose weight or feel guilty for not doing so. She made it clear that Gary's health was not her concern, but rather that he had made a promise to her that he did not keep, which signalled to her that she could no longer trust him: she wondered out loud what other promises Gary would break. This issue of trust had led Jean to initiate therapy. Gary's position was that he was doing the best he could to lose weight, although he admitted to being inconsistent in his efforts (jogging irregularly and overeating periodically). Gary felt that he had agreed to try to lose weight as a favor to Jean and was totally confused at the significance Jean now placed on this failure.

When I suggested to Gary that in the hope of mollifying Jean, he had perhaps agreed to something that he could not do, or had no real interest in doing, Gary looked expressionless, almost vacant. What I said appeared to make no sense to him. I made a mental note about how full of interpretation Jean was and how devoid of interpretation Gary was. Jean saw intent, deceit, betrayal, and failure. Gary saw unsuccessful weight loss. I wondered if their difference about this particular problem indicated a pattern.

In the hope of gaining a broader context for the presented problem, I encouraged the couple to talk about trust, their expectations of themselves and each other, and their past relationships. During the next several sessions, I learned that this was Jean's second marriage. There were several significant relationships between the marriages. Jean's first marriage ended after the birth of her second son. Both boys, aged 15 and 13, live with Jean and Gary. Jean has no contact with her boys' father, financial or otherwise, and no longer attempts a relationship with him since previous attempts have been one-sided. Jean categorized all her significant relationships with men as ultimately disappointing, finding each man lacking some essential quality that became increasingly distressing as she spent more time with him. She feared that the same was true of Gary, that his broken promise was an early sign of what would inevitably follow: her eventual disgust and final rejection of him. She seemed to be suggesting that she would rather end the marriage now with this infraction before greater disappointment followed.

This was also Gary's second marriage. Jean has been the only woman he has had a relationship with since being divorced from his first wife. Gary has a son aged 13 and a daughter aged 10, both living with their mother. Gary has enjoyed an amiable relationship with her, providing periodic financial support and frequently visiting his children. When I asked him about his former marriage, he seemed embarrassed and was uninformative about how it began and ended. After some time I learned that Gary's wife left him for another man, but Gary was unable to say what led up to that event. He reported that he had thought the marriage was good. He added that he liked being married and was glad that he had met and married Jean. When I asked Gary if he feared losing Jean in an equally mysterious way as his former wife, Gary again appeared embarrassed, but only offered, "I hope not."

During these talks about their past relationships, Jean intermittently reintroduced Gary's failure to lose weight and threatened to leave the marriage if she did not see some tangible indication that he was making good on his promise. At these moments Gary appeared lost and confused, defending himself simply by declaring that he had done the best he could. During one such session, Jean announced that she could not tolerate fussing with weight any longer, that her frustration was at its peak, and that she had to drop the subject for the present. "I think it's more important that we discuss something even worse for me — the complete absence of any demonstrated affection from Gary." Gary seemed pleased to be off the hook and oblivious to the import of what Jean had just said.

Jean became angry as she described the contrast between her present flat relationship with Gary and her previous relationships with men. She moved from tears to accusations and back again as she described her disappointment with the affectional/sexual aspect of their life together. She was furious that she had found herself "cheated" of the passion, spontaneity, and intimacy she had experienced with others. She was sad because she found herself "once more" not getting what she really needed. She then became even more distressed as she told herself aloud that perhaps this relationship with Gary was all that she deserved. I tried to interrupt this process by asking Jean who or what she was reacting to since it appeared that, whatever it was, it was not in the room. She responded, but without much feeling, that her mother had been continuously critical of her; that according to her mother, Jean was too melodramatic, too needy, too sensitive, and extremely unrealistic in what she expected from life.

As was characteristic of him during her emotional outpourings, Gary watched Jean in silence. When I asked him what he was thinking or feeling, Gary said that it was difficult for him to relate to what Jean was saying since he had no experience with what she was describing. At that point, with more anger than she had displayed previously, Jean turned on Gary for his calm and his apparent lack of connection with her. "How can I stay with a man like this!" she exclaimed.

I tried to help Gary explore what he might be feeling, a process which seemed more like teaching him a foreign language than creating a safe place for him to say aloud what he experienced internally. To my promptings, he would reply, "Yes, well, that's possible, I can see that. I could have felt that. No, I don't think I have any feelings right now." These moments were irritatingly long for Jean, watching Gary stumble around in what came so easily for her. These were certainly difficult moments for Gary too, since all his rules were not applicable here and could not help him find the "correct" answer.

I explored with Jean why she stayed in the marriage. Her answer was "safety and security"—she said she was terrified of being alone again. In addition to Gary's good salary, she appreciated things he did on her behalf to make her life easier. This very benefit, however, was also a frustration for Jean. Indeed, one of the greatest conflicts between Jean and Gary concerned "doing" for the other. Jean consistently had a list of things for Gary to do around the house. Gary would oblige, whereupon Jean usually became more depressed because it never seemed to make her feel better or closer to Gary, and often made her feel like a "demanding bitch" for asking so much. Gary reported that doing things for Jean made him feel good and that he wished Jean could just accept his giving. I attempted to create some reciprocity between them by asking Gary what he would like Jean to do for him, so she too could feel useful. Unfortunately, he could not come up with anything he needed, a response which made Jean more furious at what seemed like Gary's superior position as the one who gives but does not need. I also wondered how Gary could continuously do for Jean and not need anything in return except her appreciation, which he rarely received.

At this juncture, Gary appeared totally confused. I tried to explain how it would help if he asked Jean for something he needed, but my explanations did not work. He repeated very slowly and carefully that he wanted to do things for Jean, that this activity was what made him happy, and that he had no need of anything from her. Jean, by now tremendously frustrated, announced that she would prefer a demonstrative husband to a serf and that she was terribly unhappy.

I asked Gary where he had learned that doing for others was the way to show love. He described his family as undemonstrative but kind, as showing love by "doing." Gary's years at home until he married were spent caring for his paraplegic mother: driving her around town, doing errands, cleaning house, and being available to her at a moment's notice when Gary's father was at work. It became quite clear that Gary had been totally available for his mother, going his own way only when she had no immediate need of him. I found myself angry at both Gary's and Jean's mothers: Jean's mother for her constant criticism of Jean, Gary's mother for allowing her handicap to dominate Gary's life. I privately noted my discomfort as a feminist therapist about to lay blame at Mother's door.

Jean had no trouble seeing how she was replicating her parents' marriage in that her father was a constant disappointment to her mother as Gary was to her. She was loath to delve any deeper into that parallel for fear that Gary would get off "scot-free." For his part, Gary remained very literal, repeating whatever it was that Jean requested of him, then becoming confused about what all her fussing meant. I found speaking to this couple particularly challenging. Whenever I clarified something with one of them, I seemed to lose the other. It felt as if I had to speak two languages at once, one for each of them.

One example of my positioning myself as interpreter for Gary and Jean involved their seemingly innocent attempt to plant a vegetable garden. In her rageful account, Jean accused Gary of taking it all away from her, making her feel irrelevant and incompetent. Without apparent hurt or anger, Gary told Jean he did not see her as either one; he simply knew he could finish the job quickly while she rested. I told Jean that Gary noticed that she was tired and wanted to please her with a completed garden, like a gift he was giving her. I told Gary that Jean wanted a joint project, something to share and participate in together, that from Jean's perspective the joy would be in the process of working together. Although neither objected to my explanation, Jean expressed distress at how totally and constantly they operated on opposite tracks and how lonely she felt. Gary expressed neither sadness nor dismay, but repeated his "good intention" and said he could not understand why Jean felt the way she did.

Every complaint about the marriage was brought in by Jean: insufficient intimacy, lack of communication, dull life. Every threat and ultimatum originated with Jean: talking about other men in her past, demanding that Gary change now, idealizing a man for the future. Gary asked Jean to explain each complaint and then reminded her either that he was shy, he was different from her, or he was trying. He never became angry, disgusted, or hopeless. At my suggestion that he might be feeling any of these emotions he responded, "No, I don't think so." These exchanges typified the interaction throughout the course of therapy. Jean behaved as the stereotypical "hysterical" woman, while Gary behaved as the stereotypical "obsessional man." She yelled, cried, threatened, and reacted spontaneously, while Gary stayed contained and controlled, reacting only to literal interpretations after long silences or, quite frequently, weeks later. Whatever the content of the sessions, the process focused either on trying to "help Gary feel" or on slowing Jean's emotional rushes long enough to explore how she thought.

I suggested to Gary that he had chosen Jean for her energy, emotionality, and unpredictability to allow him to experience a life fuller than his own style permitted. I suggested to Jean that she had chosen Gary for his reserve, calm, and predictability to balance out her emotionality and to make her feel more secure. They each provided the other a richer life. Although I used this interpretation as a summary of their relationship as well as a reframe for each situation they brought to therapy, it never seemed to capture sufficiently what I had observed, nor did it adequately deal with Jean's greater expressed distress. Despite periods of diminished hostility and tension, which appeared to be the positive consequence of our sessions, Jean continued to feel lonely while Gary expressed contentment at the quiet in their home.

They each seemed so much the extreme opposite of all of their partner's traits. Did they marry each other to complete some deficit they found in themselves and come to despise the very things that had drawn them to marry? If all the complaints were from her side, did that mean he was happy? Acquiescent? Uninvolved? Was this couple demonstrating complementarity and if so what did that bode for each of them? I had attempted to use the concept of complementarity to explain their interactions, but it seemed insufficient. What had I missed? Jean and Gary, like most of us, had learned about relationships through their relationships with their mothers. How best could I use this fact in therapy? I was confused as to what direction to proceed and extremely wary of what to do with the initial information I had about their mothers. I went to the consulting group with my concerns.

Consultation

To understand the dynamic that was operating in Jean and Gary's relationship, we as consultants began to conceptualize how each spouse experienced the other. Jean experienced Gary's quietness, rationality, and reserve as intentional and painful rejection, and heard his failure to understand her thoughts and feelings as the angry criticism she had heard from her mother. Gary saw himself as inadequate in the face of Jean's emotionality, and found himself withdrawing from what seemed to be endless demands. He found himself utterly unable to satisfy Jean's demands, just as he was utterly unable to compensate his mother for her disability or his father's isolation.

We noted that this mode of analysis, familiar to therapists trained in the psychodynamic approach to family therapy, holds that partners in a marriage seek to get from one another the kind of experience they did not receive in their family of origin, and so have not internalized as part of the self. Thus Jean, who felt herself rejected by her mother, initially mistook Gary's passivity for the acceptance she craved. Conversely Gary, emotionally numbed by a childhood with a disabled, needy mother, initially saw Jean's expressivity as nurturance and independence. Each hoped to get from the other what they felt most lacking in themselves.

We supposed with the therapist that her observation of this dynamic led her to think of complementarity. Each of us shared with the therapist our stories of couples we had worked with who had interactions that resembled Gary's and Jean's. We had followed the path she had and come to a similarly frustrating impasse. We had tried to help him liven up and help her calm down in order to move them closer together. We had attempted to interpret each partner's intention to the other so each could be understood.

It seemed to all of us that the approach, not the goal, had been the error. We still wanted him to be able to experience and identify his feelings and her to be able to reflect on her feelings before speaking them but we also agreed that therapy under the aegis of complementarity had not worked. Complementarity should not be applied in this and similar cases where the part each plays is both constricted in expression, and also grossly gender stereotyped. There is too much that complementarity leaves out.

We believed that a radical shift was necessary. We needed to stop looking at the interactional system as if it were a self-maintaining entity and look instead at the individual participants. We knew that this would be a difficult move, since neither Gary nor Jean gave any indication that they would easily cooperate in individual exploration. Virtually all the sessions had been arenas for the expression of their complaints about the other and their desires for change in the other. Even Gary, though not vitriolic like Jean, merely wanted Jean to stop being angry at him; he did not see any avenues of exploration for himself.

Although desire to have one's partner do all the changing is not limited to these couples, what was characteristic here was each individual's limited knowledge of self, and relatedly their high level of projection. As long as Jean and Gary kept focusing on each other, they remained unaware of the sense of deprivation they each brought to the marriage from their childhoods, as well as the action that each could take on their own behalf. Our idea was to stop trying to see Gary and Jean's interaction as a product of complementary shaping, but instead to view their accommodation as a product of mutual projection originating from individual needs and individual history.

We suggested that the therapist assist Jean and Gary to challenge what constricted each of them and to refocus their attention to their own respective lives. Although marital harmony would make an easier life for Gary and Jean, we wanted them to do the work for the sake of themselves rather than just for the sake of the marriage. Besides, as long as they focused on each other, nothing would change.

We encouraged the therapist to see Gary and Jean conjointly to work on their individual histories with particular attention to their constricted images of themselves. As it does in most cases, this work will revolve around feelings and memories of their respective mothers. Jean's hypercritical mother and Gary's handicapped mother were, we believed, very dominant forces in shaping the assumptions and expectations that Jean and Gary were now projecting on to each other.

We believed that Alice Miller's conception of hurt, angry, or silent adults as wounded children would be the most useful approach (1981). Although Miller is not a feminist and so is not concerned as we are about avoiding mother-blame, her approach allows the child's voice to come out freely without fear that the therapist will punish the client now remembering. When Gary and Jean experience the constancy of the therapist's respectful listening without reprisal, they will with time be open to understand their mothers' stories as well as their own. First, however, their own stories need to be told so as to expose their hurts to healing.

Analysis

A key to understanding the relationship between Gary and Jean is recognizing the mutual projection system which plays a central role in the dynamics of their relationship. As typically happens in marriages based on projected expectations, each partner failed to meet the other's needs (Barnett, 1971; Kramer, 1985; Napier with Whitaker, 1974; Skynner, 1976). Struggle ensued when they tried harder to make each other satisfy these very basic needs. Jean demanded Gary's emotional expressivity and support (to be demonstrated, for instance, by his loss of weight) as proof of his caring for her. Gary wanted Jean to accept as sufficient whatever he offered so that he could feel adequate. Each needed the nurturing parenting they felt they had missed in their families of origin. She was furious that he refused to supply that need. He was deeply disappointed and surprised that she was not satisfied by what he offered.

This way of understanding how the behavior, attitudes, and expectations of two spouses fit together and cause them grief provides more assistance to the family therapist than does the notion that this is a complementary relationship. Complementarity assumes that the partners in an interaction are playing roles that fit together in a yin/yang way. "You be strong, I'll be weak." Complementarity is most useful as a way to understand and intervene when the roles are mutually beneficial, interchangeable, and temporary. When these conditions exist, the weak person gets cared for, enjoys helping the strong person feel strong, and is released from a variety of life's tasks; the strong person feels beneficent, enjoys mobility and initiative, and gains an increased sense of competence from managing tasks. In theory, if the strong one becomes ill or even pretends incompetence, the weak one will locate hidden resources and become strong.

With couples like Gary and Jean, using complementarity describes the interactional style of the couple but masks the nature of the inequality. The inequality which defines complementary interactions has to do with dominance in the interaction. One suggests, the other agrees. One acts strong, the other acts weak. When understood to be temporary and when mutually beneficial, such inequality appears harmless. In Jean and Gary's case however, the hysteric and obsessive behaviors are unequally valued in our society, and unequally rewarded. The pain was neither equal nor harmless. Jean's terror of being alone and her anger at her sense of emotional deprivation did not equal Gary's inability to feel at all.

For Gary and Jean, the inequality was also not temporary. Gary and Jean are not just fitting roles together: they are portraying core definitions of self as man and woman. His strong silent type and her maiden in distress are gender-specific, culture-wide, culture-provided, culture-ratified. Such definitions are not going to be switched by driving the system harder. Gary is not ever going to become the hysteric; Jean is not ever going to become the obsessive.

There is a third fact that makes it a problem to use complementarity to describe Gary and Jean. For someone to take the one-down position as a strategy to get one-up is a powerful maneuver. *Taking* a one-down position is not the same as *being* one-down, however. Jean *is* one-down on a number of counts: as a woman, as a constant petitioner in a relationship defined as the key to her life, and as a carrier of behavioral traits of low regard. When a one-down position is neither voluntary, strategic, nor chosen, it is not powerful and cannot be leverage to gain the one-up position. A pattern repeated in marriage after marriage in which the less-valued person displays the less-valued traits comprising the less-valued role in a non-temporary arrangement needs a stronger concept than complementarity to describe it, and a stronger approach than role-reversal to deal with it.

Psychodynamic theory helps the therapist understand that the overt emotionality of one partner and the overt rationality of the other represent different solutions to the same problem: a pervasive sense of personal inadequacy, of being unlovable. Barnett (1971) provides a comprehensive analysis of the underlying motives of couples like Gary and Jean. In line with psychoanalytic theory, he asserts that early childhood traumas shape the adult's self-concept and way of being in the world. Thus Jean, whom Barnett would describe as hysteric, survived a childhood in which she felt imploded by the affective needs of her mother, thus leaving her own needs for unconditional love and nurturance unsatisfied. She grew up seeking a mate who seemed not to have such enormous emotional needs, and could therefore accept her neediness and give to her. Her own outward appearance of vivaciousness and warmth disguised a deeply felt need for caretaking and love.

Gary, whom Barnett would label obsessional, grew up in a home where he was also unable to receive the loving acceptance he needed as a child. His mother's disability and his father's unavailability placed pressure on him at an early age to behave as an adult and to do for his mother what she could not do for herself. This early push into maturity left Gary with the appearance of a consummate adult which is actually a mask hiding a child who does not know his own feelings because he was taught to deny them.

It is exactly the outward appearance of each partner which attracts the other, and it is exactly the underlying personality structure of each which prevents the other's needs from being met. The little boy in Gary cannot tolerate the neediness of Jean. The little girl in Jean cannot bear Gary's fundamental lack of connection to her. As Barnett points out: "almost unerringly, each wounds the other in the area of their greatest vulnerability" (1971, p. 77).

While the family therapist and feminist in us may shrink from the psychodynamic labels of obessional and hysteric, it nevertheless remains intriguing and enriching to pursue the line of inquiry suggested by Barnett. How is it that the very things that attracted Jean and Gary to each other are now the qualities in each other they most despise? How are these qualities connected to unresolved family of origin issues? If one pursues this analysis, it becomes clear that the task of the therapist who works with such a couple is very delicate and involves considerable translation of each partner's messages to the other. The therapist will also be called upon to provide the acceptance and empathy to each partner that the spouse cannot yet provide.

What the psychodynamic therapists do not explain is why a man and woman, each deprived of sufficient maternal empathy, react differently—the man underinvests in relationships and pulls away from intimacy, the woman overinvests in relationships and pushes unceasingly for intimacy. An answer to this question is proposed by Philipson (1985) in her feminist analysis of gender and narcissism. She proposes that avoidance of intimacy by this type of man solves the problem of separating from mother. Separation is essential in order to become a man. If mother has difficulty accepting this separation because her son has become her vehicle for power, recognition, and achievement, she will be unable to support his move and mirror his self-assertiveness. She fails then to confirm his emerging sense of self-esteem. The double bind of such a man is that his feelings of self-worth come entirely from the approval of others, yet he avoids any real attachment to others for fear of losing his self.

Daughters of families in which maternal empathy is lacking or in which Mother cannot tolerate her child's separation will develop different characteristics than sons. This difference derives from the fact that the daughter remains identified with her mother and continues to define her self largely as an extension of Mother, rather than in opposition to her. Thus the daughter, like Jean, will grow up to be a woman who defines herself largely in relation to others and needs the approval of others to reassure herself that she is acceptable. The son, like Gary, will grow up to be a man who defines himself as separate from others, and for whom closeness brings the danger of loss of identity.

To the extent that Jean and Gary see each other as representing aspects of their own mothers, Jean will desperately want closeness, but anticipate criticism and rejection; Gary will struggle to maintain distance but hope to feel nurtured and approved. The overt desire of each—Jean's for intimacy and Gary's for distance—is so congruent with culturally expected behavior for men and women in relationships that the existence of covert expectations is rarely suspected.

Mother-blame

Over the years, psychological theory has placed the origin of a vast array of neurotic and psychotic ailments squarely on Mother's shoulders. A recent review of journal articles reports that 72 different psychological disorders have been attributed to Mother's failings (Caplan and Hall-McCorquodale, 1985). Mother-blame afflicts clinical practice as well. It is a familiar move by therapists to look to Father for amelioration of problems; in so doing, they imply that Mother has the greater share of culpability.

This aggressive criticism towards Mother with its view of her as powerfully destructive, stems from the fact that mothers are women. In every important area of human activity, woman *as* woman has been made powerless, inconsequential, and subordinate, yet in the role of Mother she is god. She has concomitant power of life and death over her child's spirit and vitality. No wonder mothers in this culture project so many of their needs on to the child: where else do they experience their power unobstructed? Children provide mothers with "someone at their disposal who can be used as an echo, who can be controlled, is completely centered on them, will never desert them, and offers full attention and admiration" (Miller, 1981, p. 35).

This power in the midst of an overarching powerlessness creates a strange and terrifying position for a woman, and a set-up for trouble: trouble for the children in continual interaction with a woman who has countless frustrations to displace and trouble for the woman who has been taught that motherhood should be her fulfillment and yet is blamed when she attempts to make it that. It is ironic that the double-bind theory was not developed to describe the position of woman as Mother in this culture. The inherent contradiction of her position produces great ambivalence. On the one hand, she is endowed with virtue and said to be all-giving and omniscient. On the other hand, she is seen as dangerously dependent, voracious, and small-minded. Mother as good is the former; Mother as bad is the latter.

It would be amazing for a society that thinks so little of women to have its children raised by them were it not for the fact that this society is also ambivalent about children. Mother-blame is not counterbalanced by a pro-child position. On the social level, only a small percentage of federal funds is spent on education, on nutrition programs for mothers and infants, on prevention and treatment programs for abuse and neglect. On the personal level, children are taught very early that adults are not really interested in how they feel or think but in seeing a reflection of what they want to see.

Since all of us are born of woman, our feelings about ourselves are inextricably connected with our relationship to a woman, our mother (Rich, 1976). How we feel about her and how we feel about ourselves in relation to her form the foundation for future relationships. For example, Jean's mother was hypercritical of her and thus Jean is hypercritical of herself and others. Jean could not sufficiently please her mother, Jean cannot please herself, and Jean cannot be pleased. Gary's mother was handicapped and dependent. Women are dependent. Jean in her dependence must be handicapped too.

Both Gary and Jean are burdened by the intensity of their relationship with their respective mothers and suffer from the absence of a relationship with their fathers. They excuse their fathers' absences as does the culture. Whereas their mothers are real individuals that they have loved and hated through the dailiness of their lives, their fathers remain remote fantasy figures available for their idealizations.

The centrality of this woman, this mother, has additional consequences. If the child is looking into the face of an unhappy woman who is furiously denying her own unhappiness, all the while indicating to her child, "You are my life," this child will learn that its life is not its own but instead belongs to Mother, as was true of her life in relation to her mother. Mother's expectations and wishes become the relevant ones, and the child learns to be inauthentic to her own self.

A further consequence of Mother's centrality derives from the fact that Mother acts as the agent of society and as such prepares her boys and her girls to assume very different places. She will prepare her boys for leadership and high regard; she will domesticate her girls. If the culture requires their feet to be bound, Mother will carry out the task. If the culture has less literal modes, Mother carries out those. In either case, she passes on to her daughter the contempt she suffers herself (Miller, 1981).

These generationally repetitive phenomena occur not because mothers are intentionally evil but because women are structured into the very center of family life without having any real power, resources, and freedom in the world. The family is the only place where most women can exercise their prerogative and influence; they do so most directly over their children. Indeed the key point at which a woman is evaluated is by her product: her children. Therefore the best marks will come if she delivers her children according to society's specifications.

It is clear then that Mother's central position and Father's peripheral position ensure mother-blame. Concomitantly, Mother's placement makes her vulnerable to being harshly judged by magnifying her personal idiosyncrasies and behaviors. Thus it is Jean's mother and Gary's mother, and not their fathers, who are the subjects behind their projections and the objects of their therapeutic exploration.

Inevitably, if a therapist creates a safe environment for clients to explore their childhood, as the therapist provided for Jean and Gary, Mother will loom large. In Jean's case, she was large and rejecting — the tirelessly critical mother. In Gary's case, she was large and needy — the fragile, dependent mother. In both instances, the child was captive. It is essential to remember that the child is captive to a woman who is, in fact, powerless in a world where power really matters. It is equally important to remember that fathers are men, and men's power is much greater in the world than is women's power, yet they abdicate this power when it comes to nurturing and teaching their children. In Jean's case this abdication reinforced her belief that her problems were caused by her mother, since it was Mother who appeared to have power in the family. In Gary's case his father's absence left him with an impoverished notion of how men behave in relationship.

To help our clients do the work they need to do, we must establish in our relationship with them a constant attention to the child in them. We must resist the temptation to categorize their mothers' behavior, because once we do so, we will betray the child. We must provide our clients with a relationship that allows them to mourn what was as well as what will never be with their mothers. Finally, we must maintain that the work is not complete until our clients first finish mourning and *then* see their mothers as autonomous selves, *then* recognize that they mothered with a deck stacked heavily against them. That part of the therapy must be informed by feminist reconceivings about mothers' relationships with their children (Bernikow, 1980; Brown, 1976; Carter, Papp, Silverstein, and Walters, 1984; Chernin, 1983; Chodorow, 1978; Dinnerstein, 1977; McCrindle and Rowbotham, 1983; Walker, 1983).

The situation is distinctly not on the brink of change. We will continue to hear only about mothers when we invite our clients to speak their childhoods until fathers are actively involved in caregiving, and until mothers are as powerful in the world as fathers.

Treatment

Goals

Our goals for Jean and Gary were:

(1) To reduce Gary's and Jean's tendency to relate to each other through a veil of mutual projections, both positive and negative, so that neither of them is seen by the other as the source of all happiness and misery.
(2) To assist Gary and Jean in honoring the child in themselves and in mourning the loss of the mother they believe they needed and did not have when they were children.
(3) For Gary and Jean to be able to accept their mothers as they are, and to be able to understand how they got that way.
(4) For Gary and Jean to expand their repertoire of behaviors beyond their usual gender role stereotypes.

Plan

Mutual projections. Gary needed to stop seeing Jean as so much like his mother that he could respond to her only in a literal, caretaking way. The therapist could lead him to look for evidence of his wife's and his mother's competence, and then help him relate to this aspect of them. Jean needed to distinguish Gary's silences and actions from her mother's disapproving looks and critical comments. The therapist could direct the couple toward these changes by invoking the names of the mothers during therapy, introducing discussion about the origin of a reaction, and weaving back into the session pieces of individual histories previously discussed.

Mourning the loss. The therapist must unequivocally validate Jean's and Gary's individual experiences of a painful or difficult childhood. Individual sessions would help Gary and Jean in the process of remembering, and in reconnecting emotionally with these memories. Both Jean and Gary were inclined to deny their experience either by minimizing the unhappiness they endured or seeing it as their own fault. The therapist might find it useful to have them bring some of their childhood pictures into the session to serve as a stimulus for a discussion about how that child appears and might have been experiencing the world at that moment. The therapist must be prepared to accept and respect her clients' anger and sadness at not getting what they wish they had.

Understanding Mother. Fortified by the experience of mourning the loss of the idealized mother they never had, Gary and Jean can begin to connect with the imperfect mothers they do have. This process may involve phone calls, letters, and visits to their mothers for the purpose of discovering who she is as a person. Tasks might include getting their mother to tell the story of her childhood or to talk about her experience as a mother, of what was most satisfying to her and what was most disappointing. Eventually it may be helpful to broaden the context for Gary and Jean so that they understand the position of Mother in society.

Gender role stereotypes. Gary and Jean are not only constricted by rigid notions of what is appropriate behavior for themselves, but they also stereotype a great deal about each other's behavior. The therapist can ask her clients to state the assumptions behind their behavior and challenge those assumptions using humor, education, and her own actions.

Jean and Gary

Jean and Gary reported what they saw as a typical stand-off. Jean said that Gary had chosen to respond to her sadness over the weekend by cleaning the garage rather than consoling her. When I asked her what she had said to Gary, she told me that she had said nothing but had clearly appeared unhappy all weekend. Since she had often told me of her desire to be massaged, stroked, courted, and spoken to, I wondered what stopped her from asking Gary for those responses. She replied that if she did ask for what she needed, Gary would merely respond in a mechanical, obligatory way which would be unsatisfying for her. I believed there was no possibility of her hearing anything until she had been validated, so I acknowledged her frustration and her loneliness and decided to return at a future session to those assumptions I believed were keeping her stuck and contributing to her unhappiness. After noting that Jean appeared satisfied, and explaining my plan to her, I turned my attention to Gary.

Gary told me that he had observed Jean's sadness during the weekend but did not know if she wanted to be with him, thus he cleaned the garage. When I asked what prevented him from asking Jean what was troubling her, he said that the question had never occurred to him. He hoped that if Jean needed something from him, she would ask.

Jean became quite angry at Gary for what she described as his total disregard for anything emotional. She said she resented him for doing tasks rather than responding to emotions. "But," replied Gary, "you do things for people you love."

I asked Gary about his first love, the one where he learned about the relationship between doing and love. Gary reiterated the various tasks he had done to help his mother and then he began to cry, showing emotion for the first time as he spoke about how very special, important, and close to his mother he felt when he was doing things for her. He described more fully the silence and distance in his family — how his father was deep behind a newspaper when he was home, and how his brother stayed just long enough to eat and sleep before running off with his wild friends, getting into trouble that seriously worried their mother. It became clear to Gary as he gave more detail to his story that satisfying his mother's needs provided a vehicle for him to experience love in an otherwise isolating family. Jean appeared moved but was eager to emphasize that she was not unable to do things for herself. I asked Jean if she thought Gary viewed her as handicapped. She said that was her impression.

Over the next several sessions, I helped Gary differentiate (1) his desire to do things for Jean from a perception of her as handicapped; (2) selected handicaps of Jean's and his mother's from total incompetence; (3) requests voiced by Jean and his mother from his own desire to respond. It seemed clear to me that Gary was unable to say no to any request made by either his mother or his wife. I wanted him to see that never saying no made his actions suspect in Jean's eyes, and also prevented him from being aware of his own needs. Rather than face the possiblity of conflict, disapproval, or rejection, Gary complied with all requests from Jean or his mother, provided he could satisfy the request by performing a task. In doing so he rationalized that his mother and his wife were handicapped and therefore he could not possibly refuse. In his mother's case the handicap was obvious. It seemed to me that Gary had applied the designation "handicap" to Jean's emotionality, interpreting her behavior as indicating a lack of emotional control analogous to his mother's lack of physical control. It would make sense then for Gary to have concluded that he could not say no to any of Jean's requests.

To help him make the necessary differentiations, and to make apparent to him the connection he was holding between Jean and his mother, I asked Gary to describe tasks that Jean and his mother were able to do. Then I asked him to elaborate on the kinds of requests made by his mother and how he had responded to them. Gary was able to acknowledge that her reliance on him was considerably greater than it had to be. When I asked Gary why he thought he had never refused his mother any of her requests— particularly since he had observed her competence first-hand and had known that his attendance was more for her comfort than absolute necessity—he became confused. He shared that he had always believed his presence was essential, otherwise his mother would not have requested it since it required sacrifice on his part. I asked Gary what he would have chosen if his presence was merely desirable rather than essential. Gary acknowledged that he would then have been faced with the dilemma of trying to figure out how to satisfy himself. I suggested to Gary that he had avoided this dilemma by maintaining the assumption that his presence was essential. This kept all other considerations, including what he may have wanted to do with his time, out of the question. I asked Gary to think about those times that his mother had asked him to do things for her when she could have done them on her own. Several sessions later, Gary reported incidents that proved his presence was desirable but not essential.

My purpose here was to assist Gary in realizing that when requests are made of him it may mean that his help is merely desirable and as such could be refused. This work with Gary continued throughout the course of therapy, weaving back and forth from memories about his mother to incidents with Jean. At the start, Jean was understandably nervous about this approach, fearing that the one thing that she could rely on in her relationship with Gary would be taken away and fearing too that Gary's refusals would sound to her like judgment against the appropriateness of her request. Only after her own work regarding her relationship with her mother was well under way could Jean appreciate this approach as leading toward honesty in their relationship.

By hearing Gary's story and witnessing his pain, Jean began to trust that Gary's desire to do things for her was not out of some position of superiority, but out of love, the kind of love that he had learned to express to his mother. Gary's sharing of information and feelings about his family helped Jean realize he was not the judgmental individual she had projected. Jean understood that not only had Gary not been critical of her needs but actually had depended on her having needs so he could express his love by attempting to satisfy them. I suggested to Gary that his actions would best be understood if he would periodically tell Jean explicitly that he was doing things for her out of love. Jean registered her appreciation of this suggestion. Gary admitted that he might find this difficult since doing without talking was a family tradition.

Although Jean began to trust Gary's intentions, after a number of weeks she "found" herself distancing from him, explaining that she just felt "shut down"—no emotion, no feelings, nothing. I suggested to her that she and Gary were beginning a major shift in their understanding and their way of relating to each other, and that perhaps she was feeling scared, confused, or disoriented. Jean claimed that her shutting down was evidence that she was a malcontent who could never be satisfied. I told Jean that my observations of her did not support this description. I also said that I believed criticizing herself was something she had learned to do long ago. I then asked Jean to talk about where she had learned to be so critical of herself. Jean described her mother as a very unhappy woman who was critical of everyone and everything, especially Jean and her needs. Her mother had claimed that Jean was overly sensitive, too needy, and demanding. The only time that Jean could remember her mother responding to her with anything approaching nurturance was when Jean was ill, as if physical illness were the only legitimate need. Jean admitted that she was ill often. She suspected that she might have purposely made herself sick as a way to legitimize her right to a responsive mother. I agreed with her that it would be very difficult to distinguish authentic sadness from the exaggerated pain that she had to express in order to be cared for. I suggested that she look for this distinction and make note of it.

I proposed to Jean that when Gary responded to her illness, sadness, or exhaustion by doing the chores, she felt tremendously ashamed, having internalized the negative messages from her mother for having needs in the first place. Rather than showing gratitude to Gary for having eased her load, she would turn on him in anger for having "caused" feelings of shame that had actually originated in her past. I directed Jean to talk about these feelings and to try to see them as her mother's feelings about her own needs. I suggested to her that her mother could not tolerate neediness in herself and so tried to censure Jean for her neediness with hypercriticism and neglect of everything except overt physical illness.

I instructed Jean to say aloud, meditate, or write at home statements that made clear those assumptions that were deleterious to her and had no place in her relationship with Gary. I also suggested that she mentally direct statements like the following to her mother: "You do not like to feel; I do." "You do not permit softness; I do." I suggested she use affirmations like the following: "I deserve response." "I want just enough." Jean had a very difficult time with this assignment and interpreted her inability to do it as an unwillingness to be responsible for herself. I reminded her that the voice of her mother was very powerful and had reentered the room at that very moment.

Judging herself caused pain familiar to Jean. What she found unfamiliar was the pain of recognizing that her needs, which had been criticized and invalidated by her mother were, in fact, worthy. At one point Jean shook her head and cried out: "If my feelings were not bad and if I wanted just enough, then why did my mother make me feel so bad about having them?" In tears, Jean recalled scenes in which her mother humiliated her, making her feelings and desires seem inappropriate or excessive. She described how such scenes never happened to her older sisters because they knew to keep their feelings to themselves, as the family required.

Jean kept struggling between the positions that her mother was right about her being an impossible child and catching a glimpse of herself as a normal child with needs and feelings. In sessions when she was able to experience herself as an innocent child, she expressed painful sadness for herself as a child whose mother was unable to respond kindly, lovingly, and unconditionally. Throughout much of therapy, Jean continued to shift between telling me that she had wanted the impossible to telling me that what she had desired was just enough. Sometimes we discussed the assumptions and consequences of each position as Jean began to recall more childhood memories. Whenever Jean began to feel guilty about her behavior as a mother to her sons, I would interrupt her and remind her that she did the best she could with what she knew, and that there would be time to deal with her own mothering when this work was further along. In truth, as Jean felt validated in our work together, she was better able to be responsive to her sons in the manner she had always hoped to be.

With my encouragement Jean began to write and call her mother to fill in some gaps in memory as well as to begin the work of hearing her mother's story. At first she asked for clarification of dates and events, then she worked herself up to ask for information about her mother's childhood and adolescence. In one phone conversation, her mother shared that she had always felt that Jean was just like her and so, fearing that "the world would get her" as she had "been gotten" assumed the responsibility to toughen Jean against expectations and hurts. She admitted to Jean that this approach had not worked, but that it was the best she had figured she could do. This part of Jean's work, though productive, had to be sporadic because it was too easy for Jean to move into such sympathy for her mother that she would end up losing herself in judgment: "How could I have been so selfish?"

We worked with deliberate slowness for myself as well as for Jean. I needed to go slowly in order to stay close to her exact experience and feelings. Any hint that I had an expectation for Jean (to do an assignment, for example) would lead us into a dangerous and dark alley of misunderstanding. A comment from me about a difference I noted about her, even though positive, would make Jean distrustful. When I asked her why, she told me that a positive comment, however nice, was still a judgment which meant that she could eventually fail. A positive comment from me also made her fearful that I would expect her to proceed in a consistently positive fashion. Jean shared how her mother had made her feel bad when she had some success or became well after an illness, telling Jean, "See, it was possible all long. That wasn't so hard." We did best when I helped Jean recall her past in order to understand her interpretations and reactions to the present.

Gary claimed no experience with feeling guilty or ashamed and found these very alien notions. I told Gary that his particular battle was with feeling inadequate, a feeling he would do almost anything to avoid. I told him that I thought his "shutting down," going numb, or showing a blank face happened whenever he determined that he could not respond sufficiently with a task. Gary concurred, citing numerous examples at home and at work where all his motivation was to avoid feeling inadequate.

Jean began to speak about her fear that Gary would abandon her as his final "no." She suspected that no human being could continue getting so little in a relationship and stay. As she described more about her fear, I heard traces of her relationship with her mother. I suggested that she speak about her experience of her mother's abandonment of her. At first, Jean had some difficulty with my suggestion since her mother had never abandoned her physically. After my validating her "feelings of abandonment throughout childhood," Jean was able to express her sadness and pain about her relationship with her mother. Her biggest battle, however, was to ward off the voice of her mother that kept telling her that she was being self-pitying, that she had no right to complain, and that her childhood was wonderful and her life just fine. During these sessions, Gary enjoyed assisting Jean to get at that voice and strike it out.

At the same time that we were doing this work, Jean came upon the book, *Women Who Love Too Much* (Norwood, 1985). As was true with many women in 1987, this book made Jean feel it had been written for her. The book seemed to give Jean greater evidence that she had been going down the wrong road in trying to have Gary satisfy her emptiness; that trying to change him so that she would feel more complete would not work. With my encouragement, Jean joined a support group based on this model, which focused on women's overinvestment in relationships with men. This served as an excellent adjunct to our work together.

Over the course of our work, projections by both Gary and Jean subsided considerably. Gary became less driven by his fear of appearing inadequate and Jean became less fearful of being criticized. Gary became more demonstrative in his affection for Jean; Jean became less excessively emotional. When Jean found herself distancing Gary, we discussed Jean's unfamiliarity with her new position. She was familiar with her roles as pursuer, rejected partner, and isolated one, but to be responded to without offering accusations, demands, or illness was very new. Gary periodically lapsed into emotional deafness, towards himself as well as to Jean, and we discussed the difficulty regarding his unfamiliarity with being accepted. Gary stopped repeating his line that Jean needed to accept him for who he was and was able to give her room to describe her needs and feelings without having either to defend himself or to dutifully act. This helped Jean, who had heard Gary's statement imploring acceptance as she had heard her mother's injunction to accept things the way they were.

Work with Gary to help him discover his feelings, needs, and wants was slow and largely unsuccessful. It was best attended to in individual sessions out of Jean's earshot since observing it generally frustrated her and accentuated her fear that she and Gary would never have a healthy relationship. Gary began keeping a journal of wishes, feelings, and needs which began as best guesses and then with trial and error became more authentic descriptions of himself.

Their recognitions of their histories and what they had missed as children permitted Gary and Jean to begin to mourn the loss of the mothers they wished they had had. After some time, Gary and Jean stopped excusing their fathers' absences and recognized how vulnerable that absence had made them to their mothers and how dependent it had made their mothers on them.

As our work continues, I hope that Gary and Jean will gain a fuller understanding about their mothers' experience in order to be more integrated. I believe that Gary will find his mother to be a competent, proud woman who did not speak about feelings but wanted to experience as little humiliation in the world as she could and so enlisted her son's aid. I hope that Gary will learn that his mother's love for him was not contingent on his "doing" for her. I trust that Jean will come to know that her mother also was criticized and humiliated by *her* mother and so had continued the culture's legacy of contempt. I hope that with time Jean will come to know her mother as a woman needy like herself. I trust that with more exploration of their mothers' lives, Gary and Jean will go even further in their understanding and acceptance of their mothers. I hope that they will go far enough to realize the fundamental impossibility of their mothers' positions—and all mothers' positions—without losing any sympathy for the child in themselves.

Pitfalls

These are some pitfalls that await the feminist family therapist in dealing with scenarios such as the one just discussed:

(1) *Saying too much too soon.* As a feminist, the therapist will not want therapy to end with Mother still seen as the villain. The clients' angry blame towards Mother must have its day, however, for it is a necessary part of the process towards understanding Mother as Subject. If the therapist skipped over that part of her own work, she would defend Mother, explain Mother, request sympathy for Mother, and untimately stand up (in) for Mother. The clients' feelings and experiences would be dismissed, and they might learn to say the right lines, but not with any heart.

(2) *Judging fairness by the clock*. By and large, it is useful to be equally responsive to both parties in marital therapy. This stance does not require equal *time* to each party, and this must be remembered. With the hysteric/obsessional couple, trying to give equal time may leave unequal pain still unequal at the end of therapy.

(3) *Trying to make him feel*. Faced with a male client who is inarticulate about his feelings, the therapist may irresistibly be drawn to the task of helping him to discover his emotions. This work will inevitably be frustrated if the man is not a willing customer. His very inability to feel likely protects him from suffering over his emotional deadness. Until *he* experiences his lack of emotionality as a problem, the therapist needs to steer clear of trying to intervene in this area.

VII
THE CARETAKING
ARRANGEMENT

From each according to her ability,
to each according to his need.

—*Margaret Atwood,*
The Handmaid's Tale

STEVEN CALLED to make an appointment for individual psychotherapy and was quite sure his problem had nothing to do with his
wife or one year old son. It "just happened" that they were the
targets of the increasingly hostile and murderous fantasies which
he had been obsessed with during the past two months. These
fantasies and the periods of overwhelming anxiety which were
sometimes associated with them comprised his presenting complaints. He believed that his symptoms were connected to his
work.

Steven was a 32 year old architect who had left a good position
with an established firm to open his own office 18 months before
seeking therapy. Although his business had been successful beyond
his expectations, he was in a perpetual state of anxiety about it and
believed that the whole enterprise could collapse at any moment.

When I asked whether he was concerned that the fantasies he
was having regarding his wife and son might lead to some violent
behavior on his part, at first Steven responded negatively. He said
he did not fear physical violence but rather loss of control over his

own thoughts. After some additional probing he admitted that for the past several weeks he had insisted to his wife that the baby not be left alone with him, lest he harm the child unwittingly.

I was concerned at this point about accurately assessing the potential for Steven's impulses to lead to violent behavior. I asked about past violence; he replied that he had never harmed his wife or child, had never been a fighter, and deplored the use of physical violence. However, he had been worried enough himself to take precautionary measures such as giving away his hunting rifle and refusing to watch any violence on television. I made a mental note to inquire directly with Sandra about this issue, but for the time being I was satisfied that Steven was not in danger of becoming psychotic or violent. His fantasies were clearly not compatible with his self-image, and he made no effort to rationalize them as being justified by any behavior on the part of his wife or son.

Steven was still sure that his family had nothing to do with the problem. Sandra, his wife of twelve years, was being very understanding and supportive, cooperating with Steven's demand that he never be left alone with the baby lest his anxiety be raised to an intolerable level. She also gave up an attractive administrative position which required some evening and weekend hours so that she could be home every evening with Steven and the baby. Steven also reported that Sandra would spend every night sleeping with her arms wrapped around him so that she could awaken and stop him if he tried to get up in the night and "do something" in his sleep. Steven presented all of this as proof that Sandra was not part of the problem and thus not necessary to the therapy.

Since it seemed clear to me by this point that Sandra was deeply involved in Steven's problem (even while sleeping), I explained to Steven that therapy could not proceed without her. An appointment was arranged for the next day. As they walked into my office the next afternoon, I was immediately impressed with the contrast in their demeanors. While they were both attractive and well-dressed, Steven had a somber, almost morose look about him, while Sandra looked quite cheerful in a determined sort of way, as if to convey the impression that there was nothing so wrong here that it could not be fixed. Sandra stated right away that she believed Steven's symptoms were a reflection of stress, and that the greatest source of stress in his life was work. Steven nodded throughout her presentation.

When I asked what solutions they had applied to the problem, Steven said he thought about it a lot and tried to understand, and avoided situations where he would be alone with his son. Sandra reported that she had been attempting to relieve Steven's pressure by not asking anything of him around the house, or asking him to help with the baby, and by doing extra things to show him that she cared about him. They agreed that none of these attempted solutions had the slightest effect on the problem.

In fact, the more out of control Steven felt and acted, the more calm, solicitous, and helpful Sandra became. I took this as evidence (later confirmed by Sandra) that she saw Steven's behavior as sick rather than bad. Steven acknowledged that he counted on Sandra's helpfulness, even characterizing her as his live-in therapist. He also admitted that he resented this helpfulness. For her part, Sandra admitted to a tendency to underestimate the extent of her own stress until suddenly she reached her limit. A bitter and vociferous fight would then ensue in which each partner accused the other of being selfish, of not caring, and of making life miserable for the whole family.

Some therapists might think of complementarity and imagine that, earlier in the relationship, the caretaking arrangement between Sandra and Steven represented a good fit: it allowed her to see herself as a giving and loving woman, and him to see himself as a loved and cared-for man. Recent difficulties had strained their resources and exaggerated their styles. Therapy could supply some adjustments in his way of making requests, and in her way of responding to them. The arrangement of who would request and who would respond would be left largely intact.

We believe that applying this concept masks a key problem, one that needs a feminist analysis. The arrangement as well as the exaggeration are produced by the struggle Steven and Sandra each have with the same dilemma: the need to be taken care of and the need not to see themselves as needing to be taken care of. The dilemma is well-known as the conflict over dependency needs.

Men deny their need to be taken care of so as not to seem weak, i.e., unmanly; women deny this need so as not to seem selfish, i.e., unwomanly (Stiver, 1984). A woman is expected to defer to others and put them first, making their needs her needs. If she is properly and typically socialized, she will develop great skill at deciphering and anticipating what others need (Miller, 1976). Since marriage is the primary relationship for most women, husbands are the chief beneficiaries of this skill. Woman as caretaker and perpetual hostess to her husband's needs is the arrangement we will examine here.

Steven and Sandra

At the end of the first session, I suggested that Steven's fantasies, troubling though they were, did seem to serve the very useful purpose of both alerting him to the stress he was under and forcing him to slow down, if only by incapacitating him with anxiety, and therefore they should not be abandoned without some consideration. I also suggested that he keep a log of his fantasies for the following session, while Sandra keep a log of her ratings of Steven's stress.

When we met again in two weeks, Steven said his anxiety had abated somewhat, but that he was becoming more aware of his negative feelings toward Sandra. I took this as evidence that Steven's fantasies had been an indirect way of criticizing Sandra. Although Steven still saw her mostly as the innocent and long-suffering victim of his anxieties, from time to time he also saw her as withholding and judgmental. His anxious, clinging episodes would be shortly followed by assertions that he wanted her and the baby to leave the house and move out immediately. Sandra would react to these episodes with fury at Steven for his seemingly endless and impossible demands. At this point, intense arguing would ensue. In spite of their apparent lack of concern, I saw the potential for dangerous physical violence to erupt during these fights, and I told them this. We discussed how to anticipate that a fight might escalate, what each of them might do when they realized that they were at their limit, and what sort of escape plans would be workable.

Over the course of the next few sessions I attempted to expand the definition of the problem to include several relational issues, such as the rigidity of the couple's roles vis-à-vis one another, their differences over involvement with the raising of their son, and expectations they had brought to the marriage from their respective families of origin, such as Steven's expectation that marriages do not last, or Sandra's that the wife is responsible for keeping everyone going. The pursuit of each of these topics was frustrated by Steven's obvious non-verbal reluctance to discuss anything that did not appear to him to be directly related to his symptoms, and not to allow any of the therapy time to focus on the needs or problems of his wife. The more I attempted to expand the definition of the problem, the more Steven insisted that it had nothing to do with anyone but himself. I found myself becoming increasingly irritated with him, and less able to truly sympathize with his plight. On the other hand, my sympathy for Sandra's dilemma was intense. I repeatedly spent time in sessions focusing on the stress she was under, urging her to notice her own needs, though it was difficult for her to recognize any needs beyond her need to be a good wife to Steven.

After two months of therapy, Steven's symptoms suddenly worsened. He became constantly plagued with violent and homicidal fantasies to the point of becoming severely depressed and virtually unable to function at work. I found myself questioning my assessment of the situation, and began to entertain the notion that Steven really *was* sick. I considered having him tested, referring him for medication, and even suggesting hospitalization. Confused, but recognizing that I myself had become part of the system maintaining the problem, I sought consultation.

Consultation

The therapist was already aware of several issues that were impeding therapy by the time she spoke to the consulting group. First, she knew that she had become more sympathetic to Sandra than to Steven, and that Steven was aware of this inequity. Second, she sensed that whenever she attempted to address a problem that was brought into the therapy session, Steven would move to a different problem. Third, she could see that Sandra's staunch determination to be helpful to her husband was somehow part of the problem-maintaining behavior that needed to be addressed.

To us it appeared that the therapist's reactions to Steven paralleled those of his wife. Like Sandra, the therapist tried her hardest to be helpful to Steven, but when he persisted in rejecting that help, or questioned its adequacy, she became irritated with him. Without attacking the positive relationship the therapist developed with Sandra, we decided to advocate Steven's position, hoping to move the therapist out of her imbalanced alignment. We imagined with the therapist the extreme frustration Steven must feel about not being understood by his wife (or his therapist). We reframed his resistance, defining it not as a fight with his therapist, but as an expression of his futile struggle to understand his frightening situation. This effort was successful in enabling the therapist to feel more empathy for Steven's plight.

With regard to Steven's seeming "slipperiness" about the definition of the problem, we proposed that Steven experienced significant anxiety whenever the therapist pursued issues beyond the point where they could be deflected with his usual defensive responses. At those times Steven reduced his anxiety by abruptly changing the subject. To stop this pattern of interchange, we encouraged her to maintain her own focus on the marital relationship and look for ways to pull him into that focus wherever she could.

In discussing what purpose Steven's symptoms might serve in the marriage, we considered two main possibilities. First, we wondered if Steven was trying to get out of the marriage but for some reason needed Sandra to be the one to "make the decision." Second, we wondered if the core issues in this marriage had to do with dependency.

As we reviewed the details of the case, we decided that Steven was very involved in the marriage and despite his hostility, had no serious intention of leaving it. In our opinion, his hostility had to do with dependency. Steven saw himself as counting on Sandra for emotional stability and even physical safety. At the same time, his fantasies indicated his anger at this dependency. Sandra was the caretaker in the relationship. In spite of all her frustrations, she had thus far not entertained the idea of being less helpful to Steven, even to relieve herself of the stress which was adding to troubles in the relationship.

We decided with the therapist that the first goal ought to be to shift the arrangement that Steven and Sandra had developed for their marriage. We recommended that Sandra be "promoted" from the role of therapist to that of wife. By upsetting this arrangement between Steven and Sandra, we thought some positive movement might be facilitated, but predicted that the first consequence of such a change would probably involve an escalation of Steven's symptoms as a means of getting Sandra to "change back."

Sandra and Steven

Following the advice of my consulting group, I spent the next two sessions reframing Steven and Sandra's relationship. I suggested that what Steven had learned from his very protective mother and grandmother was how to relate to women as caretakers. Years of being attended to for a variety of childhood illnesses had taught him that he was weak and needed to be cared for by strong women. For her part, Sandra had been raised by a woman who was the perfect model of a caretaker. Sandra's mother never had a need that she could not take care of herself, and her sensitivity to her husband's and children's needs was legendary in their family. A wonderful cook and excellent housekeeper, Sandra's mother could care for three children sick with the mumps while she canned cherries and planned the church bazaar.

I told the couple that as a result of these particular families of origin each of them grew up with a kind of learning disability: Steven imagined himself to be incapable of functioning under stress without the total indulgent support of a strong woman, while Sandra was unable to claim for herself any role in her marriage other than as her husband's caretaker, and was, consequently, acutely insensitive to her own needs. With this interpretation of their family histories as background, I said that Steven had come to believe it was Sandra's obligation as wife always to be ready to listen and advise, while keeping her own problems to herself. Sandra, in contrast, was incapable of noticing her own needs, so attentive was she to taking care of her husband. I told the couple that I wanted them both to promote Sandra from therapist to wife.

Not surprisingly, Steven and Sandra had misgivings about this intervention. Steven protested that his problems were so severe that he needed to continue being the focus of the therapy as well as the marriage. He asserted that Sandra was *not* doing such an outstanding job of attending to his needs, and all too often saw things only from the perspective of how they affected *her*. Sandra's objection to the intervention was more dramatic, for she worried that without her constant vigilance and help, Steven would become actively suicidal. Indeed, she claimed that this was the only reason she had not left him at times when he was acting crazy and abusive towards her. Steven expressed great surprise at this, and quickly asserted that he was not suicidal, and no one need worry about him on that account.

In the course of the next few weeks, some interesting changes began to take place in the marriage. Sandra came into sessions reporting that she was faithfully following my instructions and had stopped trying to solve Steven's problems. Further, when Steven presented a problem to her that she did not have the energy to listen to, she advised him to save it for therapy. She also began to notice, and then resent, that Steven was totally unwilling to listen to her problems, and routinely dismissed them as trivial. Steven was acutely aware that Sandra was changing, and to him it seemed a change for the worse. He reported that she repeatedly "shut him out" when he tried to tell her about his problems, and perceived this as selfish and punitive on her part.

Worse fights than usual began to occur with alarming frequency. Without Sandra to act as the emotional shock absorber for the couple, the spouses came head to head at each other with all the frustrations and resentments accumulated over years of their marriage. Accusations of being selfish and unloving flew back and forth. Since Steven's violent fantasies also ceased at this time, I took the fights as a sign that the conflict which had been covert and unresolvable while they were stuck in their client/therapist roles was now overt, and hoped that something good would come of this. It made Steven look and feel less crazy and freed Sandra from her fixed attention to his problems. In sessions I would try to get each of them to make "I" statements about their frustrations. Inevitably these efforts would deteriorate into something like "I feel that you are selfish." Each of them seemed stuck with a vision of their spouse as the malevolent center of their own lives.

Finally there was a crisis. An unusually fierce fight broke out in which objects as well as accusations were thrown back and forth. With their small and very frightened son as a witness, Steven and Sandra pushed and shoved each other and broke each other's most prized possessions. Their sickened awareness of their son's terror brought the fight to a halt. Steven left the house overnight and stayed with a friend. When he returned home in the morning, he and Sandra were able to have a long and painful but ultimately useful discussion about the problems in their marriage and their commitment to working them out. At the following session, Steven and Sandra reported feeling resolved about this most recent fight and feeling better toward each other than they had in weeks. They were surprised that I insisted we talk about it further. I asked for a detailed description of the fight. Both of them were uncomfortable when I labeled this fight as violent and dangerous. I told them that I was disturbed by their unwillingness to acknowledge the violence or its danger. It seemed that the extreme violence of Steven's fantasies had made both him and Sandra less able to recognize actual violence in their lives. I reminded them that violence tended to escalate over time, and warned them that if it did not cease I would be unwilling to continue working with them, since I did not want to participate in it.

This conversation had a sobering effect on Steven and Sandra. They did not like thinking of their relationship as violent, and were sufficiently impressed with my assessment of the gravity of the situation that they agreed not to have any physical contact during arguments. Still, I was concerned about the intensity of the fights and decided to seek another consultation.

Consultation

We agreed with the therapist that having the conflicts and frustrations in the marriage made more overt was a positive development in the therapy. With respect to the "promotion" intervention we concluded that we and the therapist had erred in not considering what being a wife would mean to Sandra once her role as therapist was removed. Sandra was left without any idea of an alternative function. Her withdrawal made Steven furious, yet he did not know what to ask of her as a wife other than the therapeutic caretaking he had come both to rely on and resent.

Our first suggestion to the therapist was that she work with Steven and Sandra to develop some new ideas about what a husband and wife could be to one another, focusing on mutuality, reciprocity, self-care, and care of each other. We all agreed that progress in this area was likely to be slow, since each spouse had very constricted notions of what the roles of husband and wife should encompass, and not very good models from which to draw. Further, Steven and Sandra had come to attribute to each other enormous control over their own lives. Where Steven overestimated Sandra's capacity to make him feel safe and comfortable, he underestimated his own ability to do so. Sandra underestimated her own needs and was unaware of the inevitable negative consequences of doing so. Our idea was for the therapist to work with the couple to distinguish those situations in which they could rely on themselves, versus those in which it would be beneficial to rely on each other.

In closing, we reviewed with the therapist her plan for dealing with the couple on the issue of their violence towards each other. The issue of recognizing and treating violence within marriage, particularly in its most common form of wife-battering, has been an important contribution of feminist therapists (Walker, 1979; Bograd, 1984). These writers and others have eloquently addressed the pattern, causes, and treatment of such cases, which do not need repeating here. There is another issue raised by this case which has not been much written about, and that is the matter of caretaking within the marriage. Conflict over who does what for whom in the relationship was a central problem in Steven and Sandra's marriage, and was what we focused on in our analysis.

Analysis

As we noted earlier, Sandra and Steven were struggling with the dilemma of being needy yet not wanting to be needy. This conflict within them and between them about dependency had shaped their marriage. What created this trouble for them is that they each viewed dependency as weak or bad. Their reaction is not unusual, for dependency is a disparaging word.

How has so human a need taken on such a pejorative connotation? First, dependency has been cast as the polar opposite to autonomy, the trait given top priority in Western culture. Not only are the two thought to be mutually exclusive, they are thought to reside most naturally or most appealingly in opposite sexes. Everyone knows which goes with which sex.

This division produces the second reason for dependency's bad name: making dependency a feminine trait ruined its reputation. Women are not highly valued in this society, and neither is being like a woman. In fact, to say "You're acting just like a woman" is considered an insult even to a woman, let alone to a man.

In reality, women are not more dependent than men, although their precarious economic position under patriarchy clouds this issue. They do often present themselves as needy, somewhat in the manner of a malingering child. Acting weak, helpless, faint, and confused in the presence of computers may be a good way to elicit aid and comfort, but this behavior has no connection to the actual need for another to be helpful. It is simply the standard way to relate to men, the standard way to display femininity, and the standard way to get some attention.

A third reason for dependency's bad name is that the picture of how dependency is expressed tends to be limited to clutching, clinging, demanding, insatiable, and possessive behavior. To avoid that stereotype, Steven portrayed his true dependency needs as illness, but when Sandra's ministrations fell short, he did fall back on clutching, clinging, and the rest. Such behavior, then, comes from anger and fear rather than dependency — anger about not having one's needs met, and fear that this deprivation will continue (Stiver, 1984). Anger and fear lead to the exaggerated and unattractive presentation of one's needs that further hinders their fulfillment. Both men and women are subject to these reactions because both find it difficult to accept the fact that they need, to identify clearly what they need, and to then ask forthrightly for help in obtaining it.

Responding to the needs of their husbands is a gratifying, enlarging experience for many women. They derive a sense of power by intuiting and providing what is good for their husbands. The problem is that the giving is not balanced, the expectations are not parallel, and the exchange is not mutual. In this culture, a woman is supposed to ignore her own needs. Through training, she learns to regard them as ugly, shameful, and important to restrain lest they drown herself and everyone around her. With practice at inattention, she eventually does not even know her needs. What she does know are the envy and resentment caused by this one-sided giving. These feelings are also not to be expressed directly; as a result she feels powerless. What an ironic end to what began as a source of power. Sandra knew this irony well.

Further complicating matters is an odd contradiction at the heart of women's thinking. On the one hand, they understand their primary role as caretakers to husbands. On the other hand, they view men as not being needy, as strong and self-sufficient in a way that they themselves cannot seem to attain. When women see evidence to the contrary, as they do on the rare occasions when men display neediness directly, they experience disappointment and sometimes even revulsion. Many women resolve the contradiction and bypass the revulsion by calling their men sick (as Sandra did) and therefore in legitimate need of caretaking. Other women explain away the contradiction by suggesting that their men were spoiled by their mothers, or are too busy with the cares of the world to have time to take care of themselves. Men, of course, also prefer these explanations to seeing basic neediness.

Despite her agreement to the one-sidedness of the caretaking arrangement and her effort not to know her own needs, there are times when a wife does express emotional neediness. Typically, her husband tries to be helpful by *doing* something, for merely listening with empathy does not give a man the sense that he is actively providing anything of value, and furthermore is not a highly developed skill in most men. The husband's move towards action is frequently frustrating for both wife and husband. When Sandra, for example, complained to Steven about having to work all day and then take care of him and their baby all night, Steven responded with the suggestion that she quit work. Since she knew they needed her salary, she heard his suggestion as an indication that he was not really listening. She concluded once again that her needs were not legitimate. He concluded once again that she did not really want his help.

As for his own neediness, a husband does not frequently confront it in himself because his wife monitors him so closely and gives to him so continuously. She is trained to know what he needs and supplies it as a matter of course. He takes her caretaking for granted as part of her nature, duty, and joy. Since he is saved from having to ask, he does not know he needs. Should this arrangement change, as happens when the wife gets a job or has a baby, the husband gets jealous, angry, and demanding. This outburst is not the same as identifying a need and requesting assistance. Rather according to the way the man construes it, he is simply not getting his due and lays that to his wife's being remiss, not to his being needy.

Unfortunately for all concerned, women are necessarily disappointing in their caregiving. Besides babies and jobs, they get headaches. They get tired. They get distracted. They are not always accurate in their reading of their husbands' unexpressed needs. Such times seem a great cheat to husbands; their expectations are very high and do not include vacations or lapses or even limits.

Viewing women as endlessly caretaking applies not just to wives but also to women in professional helping roles. Steven displayed this expectation with the therapist, cancelling appointments, coming late to sessions and then trying to extend the hour, calling in the evening, on each occasion assuming that his circumstances and desires were the relevant, legitimate ones and that the therapist would forgive, smooth over, and accommodate. When she held to her limits, he was always shocked and felt betrayed. After therapy sessions, he frequently complained that the therapist had paid much more attention to Sandra than to him. This too he experienced as a betrayal. If he was not getting all, he was not getting any.

It is common for men to split women into either the completely giving earthmother or the stingy withholding shrew. This image of woman as all-providing or all-depriving is carried also by women. It complicates relationships between women, including relationships between therapist and client.

What Steven and Sandra brought to therapy was Steven's symptoms which they described as frightening and out of control, circumstances indicating blamelessness and sickliness. These were acceptable to both Steven and Sandra as reasons for requiring more care. Neither manliness nor womanliness nor the caretaking arrangement had to be held up for questioning. We viewed Steven and Sandra as unable to regard dependency needs in themselves or in each other as legitimate. Therefore, these needs could not be expressed openly and directly. Frustration and hostility resulted. In our work with Steven and Sandra, we would continue to shift the framework from sickness to neediness. If their previous behavior is a good predictor, we could expect that as they speak more openly, his symptoms will decrease. The conflict between them will increase, however, for they will have to confront the terms of the caretaking arrangement.

Our vision as feminists is for both men and women to value caretaking as a worthy activity and to regard their own and others' needs as valid grounds for searching out an adequate response. We want to redeem dependency as an expectable, desirable, and reciprocal aspect of relationships. To that end, we draw on Stiver's definition of dependency as "a process of counting on other people to provide help in coping physically and emotionally with the experiences and tasks encountered in the world, when one has not the sufficient skill, confidence, energy, and/or time" (1984, p. 10). An important feature of her definition is the word "process," indicating that dependency is "not static but changes with opportunities, circumstances, and inner struggles" (1984, p. 10). When dependency is reciprocal and changing, then it can strengthen, enlarge, and create a safe atmosphere in which fun, sharing, companionship, and intimacy can thrive.

Treatment

Goals

Our goals for therapy with Sandra and Steven were:

(1) To legitimate mutual dependency for Steven and Sandra, while simultaneously encouraging each of them to develop skills of self-nurturance.
(2) To increase each partner's flexibility regarding the giving and receiving of caretaking in the relationship.
(3) To create reliable alternatives for the expression of anger so that physical violence ceased to be an option.

Plan

Dependency. Through therapy Steven and Sandra became aware of their dependency on each other, and they found this difficult to accept. The therapist could help the couple redefine dependency in a more positive way by ensuring that it was mutual, and that each partner had explicitly consented to be depended upon. One of the reasons that dependency took on such large and ugly proportions in this marriage was that Steven and Sandra both tended to underestimate how much they could do for themselves; each spouse consequently saw the other as having total control over who would be taken care of in the relationship. The therapist could point out opportunities for Steven and Sandra to rely on themselves, as well as on each other, for nurturance and care.

Flexibility. The rigidity of their roles vis-à-vis caretaking left Steven feeling sick and needy while Sandra felt resentful and depleted. Both needed to enlarge their capacity for giving and receiving care from the other. The difficulty here was that Steven and Sandra saw their positions as firmly rooted in human nature. The therapist could assist them in shaking loose this belief by exploring how those roles developed in their respective families of origin, particularly focusing on how well they have worked for significant family members. Tasks could be assigned which forced each of them to try out the other's predominant role, or conversely, which exaggerated these roles to the point of absurdity.

Anger. Although Steven and Sandra did not think of themselves as a battering couple, their fighting occasionally led to physical violence. The therapist, sensitive to both the denial and the pattern of gradual escalation which are typical of marital violence, could keep this issue on the table by insisting on hearing about escape plans, signs of escalation, and detailed accounts of the exact type and extent of physical violence in the couple's fights. In this marriage, one of the precursors of violence had been the build-up of undiscussed and unresolved anger. The therapist could prescribe smaller, more frequent fights, teach techniques of fair fighting, help the couple to identify anger as it occurred in the sessions and deal with it there.

Sandra and Steven

A calm followed the crisis for this couple. For several weeks Steven and Sandra dealt with each other gingerly, and did not demand or expect a great deal from one another. I used this time to talk about expanding their vision of what husbands and wives could be. I urged them to keep the caretaking aspect of their relationship strictly at the level of conversation right now because of their recent fright and because of their tentativeness with each other. I thought this was a good time for them to work on self-care and suggested that they each begin taking small steps to care for themselves. One evening Sandra asked Steven if he would like to see a movie with her. She selected the film, checked out the show-time, and went to the bank to cash a check so they would not be short on cash. Steven reported that the evening had been fun, and different from their usual excursions in that typically Sandra would voice her interest in seeing a particular film, but would leave it up to Steven to take the initiative for arranging to see it.

Not long afterwards Steven decided to take an afternoon off from his hectic work schedule to go golfing with a friend. When I commented on how unusual it was for him to interrupt his work schedule for any personal reasons, his only explanation was that he was getting worn down by his business and "owed it to himself" to relax once in a while.

Neither of these events was of monumental proportions, but they stood out clearly against the usual background of Steven and Sandra each seeing the other as having control over their own well-being. I asked them to report any further developments like these to me, and cautioned that it might only be a fluke, and that they would soon fall back into their usual pattern of one-sided care-taking.

During this phase of therapy, I found it hard to keep the momentum going. Both spouses had been badly frightened by the revelation of the intense anger they felt for each other, and had pulled back to avoid another such crisis. It was difficult to engage them in any topic which was even mildly conflictual. Steven was more explicit on this subject, stating flatly that he was not willing to risk another crisis, and wanting to discontinue the marital sessions in favor of individual therapy until things "cooled off." I told him that

I believed he was holding me responsible for the crisis and suggested that his unwillingness to take any more risks in therapy right now indicated a lack of trust in me; he might see my relationship with Sandra as a betrayal of him. Further, I speculated that this was an error Steven was prone to make about women, that from his experience in his family of origin he had come to expect women to betray or fail him. Without missing a beat, Steven asked, "Do you think I should call my mother?"

Steven's question marked the beginning of a shift in the therapy in which we spoke at greater length and in deeper ways about the families in which he and Sandra had grown up, and how their early experiences exposed them to models of adulthood and married life whose influence continued to be felt. These conversations were stilted at first, as both Steven and Sandra continued to speak about their families in idealized, protective ways. We did genograms of each of their families, which proved to be very useful. As we looked back at the roles men and women had taken on in their families clear patterns began to emerge. Sandra was descended from three generations of women each of whom had been the caretaking partner in their marriages. The prevailing myth in Sandra's family of origin had been that women were the backbone of the family. In the two generations before her Sandra's mother and grandmother had married men with significant physical limitations. These men were catered to and cared for by their wives, who never complained about their burdens, and shouldered most of the real responsibility in the family.

Sandra had been determined to choose a different kind of man for herself. When she met Steven he seemed ideal. Strong-willed and ambitious, creative and somewhat flamboyant, Steven looked like the sort of man who would never fade into the woodwork, never require the sacrifice from her that she had seen her mother and grandmother make for the men in their lives. What she had not seen then, and only began to understand during therapy, were the similarities between Steven and her father, and between her mother and herself.

Steven was even more reluctant than Sandra had been to discuss his family. He voiced concerns that focusing on the past would be a dead end, would waste time, and might even make things between him and Sandra more difficult. Eventually I had to rely on my authority as the "expert" to persuade Steven to engage in a discussion about his family.

Most of the facts Steven reported in discussing his genogram had already been reported earlier in the therapy. This time we focused on the feelings he had then and now as a member of a violent family. This task was very difficult for Steven, as he had emotionally cut himself off from his family years before. Stories about the violence he had witnessed as a child — his father's abandonment of the family when Steven was three, his mother's subsequent depression, his parents' alcoholism, and his grandmother's anger at having to take care of three little boys — would be told in a flat, monotone voice. I had to prevent myself from rescuing Steven by anticipating his feelings, and also prevent Sandra from doing the same thing. I wanted to present to Sandra a way of listening to her husband's problems without feeling obligated to solve them. Sometimes I would move my chair close to hers and confess that I was having to struggle against the temptation to rescue Steven, and I would ask her help in not doing so. She and I would consult with each other about how to respond to Steven in a way that expressed support but did not rescue. This consultation was done in Steven's presence, and he would watch, totally fascinated, as his wife and I talked together about how difficult it was for us to express support and concern for him without taking over his problem and fixing it.

Over a period of several months, Steven and Sandra began to appreciate how their families of origin "fit." I asked each of them to talk with members of their families of origin. Sandra learned that in spite of her mother's reputation as the powerhouse of the family, her mother feared getting older and becoming crippled with arthritis. Sandra also learned that her mother had long suffered from bouts of depression which she kept hidden from her family. That her mother could feel vulnerable was a revelation to Sandra, and was taken as permission to experience her own needs as legitimate for the first time. She began to enlarge her definition of wife and woman to include attention to her own needs.

Steven was more hesitant than Sandra had been to reconnect with his family. He remained very protective of his parents, not wanting to "dredge up the past" for them and not wanting to believe they were still relevant in his life. Finally, he decided to talk to his older brother. Over the course of several conversations

Steven learned that the violence in his family had been much more widespread and enduring than he remembered. His brother told him that their father had not only beat their mother when he was drunk, but had also "punished" the two older boys with severe spankings. Steven was spared this abuse because he was young and also because he was sick a great deal of the time. By the time he was three their father had left the home. Steven also learned that his father had undergone treatment for his alcoholism several years earlier, and had re-established contact with his two older sons since then. He had not attempted to contact Steven because Steven had always seemed to "belong" to his mother. Steven learned that none of the three sons was in regular contact with their mother. His brother told Steven that he always felt angry and sad around their mother, and that it was therefore easier to stay away. Steven experienced a strange sense of relief to realize that his feelings about his mother were so similar to his brother's.

For me, doing family of origin work with the couple was by far the most rewarding part of the therapy. Each contact with their families seemed to yield new information which made their particular marital arrangement more comprehensible to them and to me. Each of their families had exaggerated the typical male-female split regarding caretaking and dependency. Sandra's highly competent mother had cared for her husband and children for years without complaint, not even noticing her own needs and desires. In Steven's family an abusive, and then completely absent, father contrasted with his intensely involved mother and grandmother.

Slowly things began to improve for Steven and Sandra. Steven's anxiety attacks became less frequent, and less frightening to him. His relationship with his son improved, and he felt more confident at work. Between Steven and Sandra there were small changes. She began to take regular time for herself, away from Steven and the baby, to "treat herself." This was first done in the form of an assignment, but later became part of Sandra's week. They both made strides in being able to listen empathically to the other, without feeling a demand to solve each other's every problem. I assigned them the task of having smaller and more frequent fights, and taught them the techniques of fair fighting. Their fights became less explosive and ceased to include physical violence.

I tried to redefine dependency to Steven and Sandra in as many ways as I could. We discussed the ability to be sometimes vulnerable and dependent on one's spouse as a survival skill and a virtue. I assigned tasks which required Steven and Sandra to depend on each other in small ways. Sometimes I asked them to temporarily reverse their predominant roles: for Sandra to try out being needy, and Steven to practice being depended on. At other times I had them exaggerate their predominant roles to the point of absurdity. These efforts had the cumulative effect of loosening the rigidity of the couple's roles vis-à-vis caretaking.

All of this change occurred gradually and with frequent backsliding. Both spouses agreed that it was sometimes easiest to do what they knew best, and so occasionally Steven would get depressed (or anxious, or upset, or just grumpy) and Sandra would try to "fix" him. It was still difficult for Steven to accept Sandra's neediness without feeling anxious that she may not be there for him if he needed her. Steven was still largely cut off from his family of origin, and Sandra had not resolved her anger at herself, Steven, her family and the cosmos for all the years she spent caring for everyone but herself. Therapy continues, although sessions are more spaced out, and less volatile. There is still more that Steven and Sandra want from their marriage, but every once in a while now they feel like celebrating what they already have.

Pitfalls

These are the pitfalls that await the feminist family therapist in working with couples in a caretaking arrangement:

(1) *Coming down with terminal gratitude.* A feminist family therapist, like a non-feminist family therapist, may have a long stretch from one male client to the next who speaks about his feelings. Upon seeing this kind of man, the therapist may be so relieved and appreciative as to conclude that success has been achieved and nothing more need be required of him. Thus the therapist betrays (and probably parallels) the wife, thinking the husband has done more than should really have been expected merely by expressing some emotional vulnerability. If left un-

checked, this reaction will lead the therapist to teach the wife to ask for less as the husband is encouraged to speak up more.

(2) *Being ready to expose and destroy.* The feminist family therapist is ripe for fury at a man whose behavior is best described as passive, manipulative, and needy. Her anger is fueled on behalf of his wife who, as a consequence of interacting with him, generally seems confused and mystified, but is still trying to take care of him. The desire to expose his pranks as such leaves the therapist unsympathetic to him and blinds her to the systemic component.

(3) *Falling into The Great Divide.* The all-providing/all-depriving split which afflicts people's expectations about women affects the therapist's view of herself even though as a feminist she may be eloquent in its rebuttal. With families in which woman's role as caretaker is an especially salient issue, the therapist may be pulled from one extreme to the other with dizzying speed. When she stops the switching, she may spend some time disoriented with nothing underfoot before she regains her own place.

(4) *Leaving out the bad part.* Teaching people to speak up about their own needs for caretaking is tricky business. They usually have to work so hard to be able to express what they want that once they do, they think they have won the battle. They are then shocked not to get what they requested, and are enraged at being ignored or rejected. At the beginning the feminist family therapist must tell her clients — *especially* the women clients — that they have two struggles in front of them, not one.

VIII
THE LESBIAN COUPLE

The rules break like a thermometer,
quicksilver spills across the charted systems,
we're out in a country that has no language
no laws, we're chasing the raven and the wren
through gorges unexplored since dawn
whatever we do together is pure invention
the maps they gave us were out of date
by years.

—*Adrienne Rich,* The Dream of
a Common Language

WE COULD RECOGNIZE them as brave women, spirited women, and loving women, but instead they are said to be perverted, criminal, ill, insane, sinful, deviant, depraved, and deprived. They are called old-maid, witch, butch, dyke. The homophobia and hatred reflected in these words permeate not only personal belief and cultural values, but professional theory as well. The literature of family therapy, for example, makes lesbians[1] invisible by what we must regard as malevolent neglect. Two recent articles are welcome exceptions to the general pattern of ignoring lesbian existence (Krestan and Bepko, 1980; Roth, 1985). Equally troubling is the fact that some of the most widely used theoretical concepts in family therapy would pathologize a lesbian couple by fiat if we applied them.

In contrast to a pathologizing point of view, some lesbian feminist writers offer a highly idealized version of the love relationship

[1]We use the term lesbian in this chapter to refer to women who have adopted that term for themselves.

between two women (Lewis, 1979). They describe the lesbian couple as attempting, though admittedly not always succeeding, to respect individual needs of the partners even when these needs seem potentially threatening to the relationship. The aim of each partner is to rise above the jealousy, possessiveness, and dependency which those writers believe is prevalent in heterosexual couples as a result of the assumption of male ownership over women. Thus removed from the dictates of romantic love which engender passive swooning heroines and active rescuing heroes, lesbian love claims to be born of friendship and mutuality.

Idealized versions of the dynamics which bind partners to one another are no more useful for our work than pathologized versions but, as an opposite pole, they do point up the long distance we have to travel to reach a balanced perspective. Family therapists—feminist or not, lesbian or not—must know ourselves and our therapy to be profoundly influenced by attitudes of aversion towards women loving women. Our own struggle against these attitudes is the prerequisite to any salutary work with lesbian couples.

Kim and Kathy/Ruth and Rita

Kathy and Kim had been live-in lovers for over fifteen years. They were both employed as administrators in separate departments of a large insurance company. For the last five years of their relationship, they had been in and out of therapy, working on issues of finances, professional dilemmas, and most often, sexual infrequency and/or disinterest. Their most recent request for help had to do with their mutual desire to "re-evaluate the entire relationship." They came in shaken and fearful that "this time, the relationship is really in trouble." Their questions and doubts were related to new romantic attractions they both felt toward another couple, Ruth and Rita, who had been their long-standing friends.

Ruth and Rita had been live-in partners for eight years. Ruth recently became a CPA and was working for a mid-size public accounting firm. Rita had supported Ruth through graduate school by working as a secretary and was currently a full-time student pursuing a degree in medical technology. The two couples had a common network of friends in their community, and over the years they had offered support and nurturing to one another for various personal and professional dilemmas. Besides spending a good deal of time in each other's homes, they shared parties, business ventures, and political causes.

By the time Kathy and Kim came in to evaluate their relationship, Kathy had started a sexual relationship with Rita. Kim and Ruth were attracted to one another, but most of their emotional energy seemed to be going toward grieving the losses in their primary relationships. There were no secrets among these women and so all four had information about attractions and behavior of one another. Soon after Kathy and Kim came in to talk, Rita and Ruth called for therapy, also wanting to evaluate their relationship.

In my session with Kathy and Kim and in my session with Rita and Ruth, I heard how these women were reaching out emotionally to one another as well as to women outside the foursome, looking for comfort regarding their distress over troubles in their original relationships. Some of these comforting relationships became sexual and thus upsetting to other intimates. I heard how the women's community rallied around with support and advice. My reaction was a mixed one as it had often been with other lesbian couples in therapy. On the one hand, it was clear to me that these sexually open relationships were problematic and a source of pain for all four clients. I was drawn to focus on what seemed a serious disregard for boundaries: boundaries around self, relationships, homes, and information. I began to think in terms of "triangled" and "fused." On the other hand, I admired the active and loving concern these women demonstrated towards one another and honored the courage which enabled them to "go that hard way together. . . ." (Rich, 1979, p. 188). Pulled between a pathologizing perspective and a respectful one, I presented my perplexity to the consulting team.

Consultation

As feminist family therapists, we know that women are often labeled as pathological simply because their behavior, values, or feelings do not conform to the expectations of male theorists and clinicians. Because we are committed to an understanding of our clients free from such sexist bias, it concerned us to realize that the therapist's assessment of these women as triangled, fused, and disrespectful of boundaries made sense to us. We thus began the consulting process by posing a question for ourselves and the therapist. What assumptions about relationships and sex were producing our opinions about these clients' situations? A brief discussion brought out several specific assumptions under which we were operating: that stable relationships are dyadic and have clearly defined boundaries around them, that friendship should be asexual and distinct from a primary relationship, and that monogamy is preferable to any of its alternatives. We thought it possible that such assumptions emanate from heterosexism, a view that holds heterosexuality as the only legitimate form of sexual identification. A different view might create a different set of assumptions about primary relationships. We wanted to leave this possibility open for our consideration rather than have it closed arbitrarily by prejudice. Heterosexism has informed the development of cultural and individual value systems as well as family therapy theory; we intended to stay alert to signs of that bias in our thinking.

After further discussion together, we decided that working with these relationships as one system would offer additional options for therapeutic leverage and thus we planned the next steps: (1) invite all four of the women to participate together in conjoint sessions; (2) use a member of the consulting team as a co-therapist; (3) gather information about the nature of the boundaries and rules of this system; (4) inform the clients of this interest and share observations with them; and (5) consider non-pathological understandings of the way this system functioned.

Kathy, Kim, Rita, Ruth

All four women agreed to attend a conjoint session. Kathy and Kim were still living together as were Ruth and Rita, although in neither case were the housemates still intimate or sexual. Rita was contemplating finding her own apartment; Kathy was doing the same. Kathy and Rita said that they had gravitated toward each other for mutual support and then evolved into lovers. Ruth and Kim said they felt abandoned.

We listened to the content that these women brought into the session: sexual disinterest, ambiguous loyalties, financial disagreements, feelings of being unloved and misunderstood. The flow of details and the descriptions of all the alliances—present, past, and potential—caused us to parallel the very process of feeling confused and being overwhelmed that we observed in our clients. We had to remind ourselves to be open to observing this system as it presented itself and to avoid judgments about the changing connections.

What made that openness especially difficult was the way that these women presented their concerns to us. They appeared to have absorbed society's lesson that their lives were "pathological" and they came to tell us about the pathology. We told our clients that we admired the commitment and courage they demonstrated by agreeing to work together in therapy. We said that they seemed to be experimenting with different ways of organizing relationships and asked them to tell us about their experience of themselves. Acknowledging to them that there was value in what they were doing seemed to shift their thinking. They began to talk about their behavior with more respect and described themselves as striving to make choices which were for the good of themselves and one another.

We commended the women for their continuing interest in and support of each other, and pointed out that such a thing could not occur where couples are more isolated from others. At our request, all four women agreed to return in two weeks in order to see where things appeared to be heading and to discuss what was happening to each of them. Both of the original couples stated that the relationships they had been in were extremely important to them and they wanted to understand what had happened to them.

At the next session and in several succeeding sessions, we observed behavior which demonstrated difficulties the group was having with conflict resolution, sexual coupling, decision-making, and caretaking. Rita and Kathy decided to move out of their respective homes and move in together. Telling about this change had little observable emotional impact on the four women involved. Ruth expressed some sadness at the loss of Rita, but the others spoke of the change as if it were a temporary readjustment of alignments rather than a permanent separation.

We asked about feelings of abandonment and proposed that some "leaving" had been happening for a while in the form of one person's disappointing the other, rejecting the other, ignoring the other's concerns, and so on. At this suggestion Rita and Kathy became tearful. Kim appeared unmoved. We encouraged the four women to talk about their reactions, suggesting that the session could be used as a supportive and structured place to speak about thoughts and feelings that were likely even more difficult to discuss outside the session. Little response came, and we said that perhaps more time was needed for each one to examine her own response before sharing it with others.

At the next session, Kim, Kathy, and Rita reported that they had slept together. Kim said she had liked sleeping in the same bed with Rita and Kathy, but had become very upset by their sexual advances, which she had refused. She was unable to articulate what most upset her. She did not think the idea itself was the problem, for she had been a part of a sexual threesome from time to time and still maintained an interest in group sex. Ruth admitted feeling upset that she was not included. All members of the group told of experimenting with multiple sexual partners, describing these instances as attempts to keep from losing anyone or leaving anyone out of their lives. After remarking upon the continual fluidity of the women's relationships, we asked the women to consider for the next session what values, in addition to what they had already mentioned, were available to them in threesomes that were absent for them in their previous grouping into dyads. In this way, we stayed with our plan to avoid judgmental statements. Once the clients gathered more information for themselves, we could suggest a discussion about the gains and losses of relating in various configurations.

Second Consultation

With the information obtained in the group sessions, the therapists returned to the consultants to discuss their current assessment and to plan further treatment. The therapists reported that in answer to the query about threesomes, each of the women had described herself as terrified of exclusion. Each woman said that she wanted to do what was best for herself, but not hurt another; if another should express hurt or disapproval, then the aim would be to redo the original decision until mutual accommodation could be found.

Again, the consultants as well as the therapists struggled with the fundamental challenge to our usual ways of thinking—both personally and clinically. As we looked to family therapy for help, we realized that our training would lead us to see inadequate boundaries in this system, and to apply the term fused to these women. Yet we know that theory determines what can be seen and if we adopted a different theory, we would see something quite different. For example, boundaries might recede in importance and relatedness emerge more prominently.

We faced a similar question about theory when we tried applying the concept of triangles to these relationships. According to the common usage in family therapy, triangles represent the effort of a dyad to avoid direct conflict by involving a third person to take sides or become a scapegoat. It was certainly true that members of this system did not resolve conflict well, but was that *because* they involved more than two people in their struggles?

The therapists were presented with a situation which afforded them the opportunity to pursue these issues. Immediately prior to the consultation, Kathy and Ruth independently called the therapists requesting individual sessions. We debated whether this request represented progress towards recognizing individual needs, or an effort to draw in a third party (the therapist) to alleviate a conflict with another member of the group. Since we had no evidence that the clients were making gains in dealing with conflict directly, we decided on the second interpretation. For the present we advised the therapists to insist that issues relevant to relationships within the group continue to be dealt with in the group.

As we moved towards making the treatment plan for subsequent sessions, the therapists assessed that the best thing they had done was to maintain a stance of noninterference in the system long enough to allow some patterns to emerge. It had been a difficult stance because the therapists did see much behavior and history that would ordinarily be called pathological. The therapists resisted temptations to pull individuals prematurely out of the group for family of origin work, or to draw boundaries arbitrarily around dyads and engage them in couple counseling. The thera-pists agreed that this stance would have been altogether impossible were it not for working as co-therapists, each keeping the other from becoming too involved with any one member of the group.

We discussed two issues as priorities at this stage of therapy: finding effective ways of resolving conflict, and addressing individ-ual needs by identifying them, speaking them, and managing re-sulting consequences. The team discussed these issues as being particularly loaded for women. We know the enormous cost to women of their typical adaptation in these areas. We also want to remember that there are distinctive aspects about living as lesbians that shape the way women's issues and human issues are experi-enced and incorporated.

Analysis

There are many dimensions to consider in working with lesbian couples. We recommend instructive references (Abbott and Love, 1977; Baetz, 1980; Gartrell, 1984; Goodman, 1980; Hidalgo, Peterson, and Woodman, 1985; Krestan and Bepko, 1980; Loulan, 1984; Rich, 1980; Roth, 1985; Vida, 1978). Also, we urge special care in selecting supervisors and consultants. Here we will only have space to discuss those four aspects particularly rele-vant to our work with the presented case.

Heterosexism/Homophobia

American culture is heterosexist. Discussion regarding universal bisexuality, hormonal determinism, or nature versus nurture ob-scures this fundamental point: Heterosexuality serves as the linch-pin in the patriarchal structure and functioning of our society. That is to say, heterosexuality has been "imposed, managed, or-ganized, propagandized, and maintained by force. . . . " to ensure that women are physically, emotionally, and economically depen-dent on men (Rich, 1980, p. 649). Women who remove themselves from the ranks of the available are met with all the diagnostic, medical, legal, religious, and social power at the disposal of those who suffer their loss and resent their nerve. Widespread homophobia is a grim tribute to the success of the campaign and to the threat of reprisal that accompanies it.

Heterosexist bias is a major problem for the therapist working with lesbian clients. So pervasive is the bias, so automatically does it guide thinking and with such familiarity, that the therapist continually risks projecting it into the therapy or becoming paralyzed into inaction for fear of doing so. To complicate matters further, our homophobia may match the clients' own. We will then miss it entirely. We may think that we are successfully offering our clients empathy and understanding when we are actually and unknowingly supporting their own self-hatred. For example, it is homophobia that leads a therapist and her lesbian clients to attribute disturbances in a relationship to lesbianism rather than to the often disabling impact of prejudice. Such occurred when Kim and Kathy first presented their sexual problems in therapy. Kim wondered if women could really remain sexually interesting to her over time, since there is no stark anatomical contrast. The therapist wondered also. The revulsion toward sex between women that Kathy and Kim and the therapist had been taught should have been considered as the possible source of the problem.

Problems in Daily Living

Lesbian couples have conflicts over the same issues as do heterosexual couples: money, closeness, sex, and tasks. Ruth and Rita for example frequently argued about finances, and they as well as Kathy and Kim had difficulty with closeness. Sex was the salient issue between Kathy and Kim. Kathy wished for more frequent and passionate love-making, while Kim demonstrated little interest except to oblige Kathy. Allocation of household tasks was somewhat less troublesome for these couples than for other lesbian couples we have seen, primarily because they had been together long enough to have reached a workable agreement.

In each of these traditionally conflictual areas, the lesbian couple must establish its own creative solution. Roth discusses distinguishing features of that effort and we recommend her paper for its descriptions of the patterns and pressures in each conflictual area (Roth, 1985). Here we want to hold up two factors which complicate the process of finding solutions *in general* for lesbian couples.

One complicating factor has to do with models. Whereas the heterosexual couple can call upon families of origin in memory or in fact, this resource is rarely useful to the lesbian couple because heterosexual couples typically base their arrangements on gender role stereotypes. (A small proportion of lesbian couples do adopt highly differentiated roles modeled on heterosexual gender role stereotypes. The majority of lesbians, however, do not adhere to rigid role behavior.)

Other sources of models widely available to heterosexual couples—magazines, newspapers, self-help books, formal courses, and television programs that give covert or overt lessons on managing a partnership for living—are based on assumptions about arrangements, outlooks, and supports that generally do not apply to lesbian couples. Although it may be an advantage to have the freedom to design one's own solutions, that freedom entails losing the sense of certainty and direction found by following tradition and receiving attendant social validation.

The second factor complicating the lesbian couple's effort to resolve daily problems derives ironically from the very feature that can make the relationship so enjoyable. That is, the relationship consists of two women. Like other women in this culture, a lesbian has been socialized to be more concerned with the feelings of the other than with her own, more responsive to the needs of the other than to her own. Since in a lesbian relationship the other is also a woman, each partner finds herself receiving a degree of attention unknown in her relationships with men or family members where women are expected to be the unilateral givers. The sensitivity to one another between the partners in a lesbian relationship can bring deep pleasure and well-being. At times, however, it has troublesome side effects. In her novel *Other Women*, Alther characterizes such an outcome in her description of the long-term relationship between Caroline and Diana:

> Their relationship wasn't working, they finally concluded, because each had an equivalent need to be needed. . . . [W]ith each other life was a constant struggle to outnurture. . . . Each put on ten pounds from the candies and pastries the other brought home, which were dutifully devoured to please the donor. During lovemaking each would wait for the other to climax first, until both lost

interest altogether. They fought over who got the most burnt toast, or the lukewarm second shower. . . . Eventually they were compelled to address the issue of what to do about two people in whom thoughtfulness had become a disease (1984, p. 16).

How does such thoughtfulness make problem-solving difficult? It impedes the capacity to be aware of one's own needs and even if aware, to voice those needs in the clear terms that may *create* conflict, but also make possible the explaining and negotiating that can *resolve* conflict.

The Lesbian Community

Members of the lesbian community may well comprise the primary interactional context for the lesbian couple. In therapy (and in hospital visitation, insurance policies, courts of law, funerals, banks, etc.), the relevance of these friends is usually disregarded. We point out their relevance because they serve not only as primary relationships but also as sanctuary and identification.

Anywhere that lesbians congregate can become a sanctuary: a woman's music concert, a political rally, a woman's bookstore. Numbers create for the moment a sense of place where the heterosexual majority is not intruding, watching, and ready to condemn and possibly persecute. As all oppressed people use their group affiliation to help them exist in a hostile world, lesbians too embrace their group identity as a way to survive hatred. They create a proud identity by drawing upon the characteristics that make them unique and strong, finding positive images in women's song and literature.

Lesbian women look to the lesbian community for fellowship, sisterhood, family, and kindred spirits. Those women most connected to the community are aware of the norms that particular lesbian community expects of its constituency. For example, some lesbian communities may expect couples to be monogamous, while other communities may hold monogamy to be oppressive. The most influential community for the four women discussed in this chapter shifted from a closed group of ten couples to an open group with couples, singles, and former lovers. This shift took place several months before the women sought therapy, and it is this context too that needed to be considered as part of the entire picture.

Traditional Concepts from Family Therapy

Several core concepts in family therapy, such as triangle, fusion, and boundary, might well come to mind to describe and explain the distinct patterns and characteristic problems of lesbian relationships. These three concepts are imbued with heterosexist bias, and application of them to any relational system may yield a distorted view. In particular, application to lesbian relationships will inevitably result in a pathologized and impoverished description.

Triangles. In the lesbian system described in this chapter, the number of overlapping threesomes was certainly noteworthy and pulled the therapists toward analyzing interactions from the traditional view in family therapy that triangles are always perverse (Haley, 1971). Drawing in a third person may sometimes create a perverse triangle, but what grounds are there for saying that sometimes it might not? First, given the web of relationships lesbians tend to sustain, the primary unit relevant to a specific conflict which appears to be a dyadic problem may well be three persons, four, or more. Further, we may be looking at an expression of women's psychology. Gilligan (1982) proposed that, in contrast to men's way of applying an impartial principle to resolve a moral dilemma, women cast a wide net of relational concerns, giving attention to every affected party. Perhaps the same is true about women's way of resolving conflict.

Second, we know that managing conflict in a productive way is difficult for everyone, but is especially difficult for women. Because they have no power base in the real world, women, both lesbian and heterosexual, are used to dealing with conflict only in indirect ways (Miller, 1976). Pulling in a third person or several other persons does make confrontation less direct, but doing so may also make the confrontation possible at all. Diluting intensity so that anger can be managed without loss of the other person is the desired and facilitated effect.

Fusion. In family therapy, fusion figures prominently as an explanatory principle in the two major articles on working with lesbian couples (Krestan and Bepko, 1980; Roth, 1985). Thus in conceptualizing our work with the clients presented in this case, we wanted to examine the meaning and usefulness of the concept of fusion. The difficulties that we found with the concept here led us to question it altogether.

In family therapy, fusion is most closely associated with the work of Bowen (1966), who uses the term to anchor the lower end of a continuum measuring an individual's capacity to act and feel as an independent self. People who suffer from "ego fusion" have poorly defined ego boundaries, are excessively dependent on the opinions and approval of others, and have great difficulty speaking on their own behalf. At the upper end of the continuum are differentiated people who have a clearly defined self, think and feel independently of the needs and desires of those around them, and make decisions based on rational rather than emotional grounds. The term fusion is also applied to relationships. According to the theory, a person whose emotional and intellectual systems are fused will "fuse into" relationships, i.e., will "lose self" (Kerr, 1981). We found that if we applied the concept of fusion to Ruth, Rita, Kathy, and Kim, we did see some fit. These four women do seem excessively reactive to each other, are intensely close, and have difficulty taking positions which might incur disapproval.

Nevertheless, further thought led us to question fusion as a way of explaining clients' behavior. The term describes a person who places a higher priority on the maintenance of the relationship than on self-expression, self-development, and even self-health. For the fused person, the distinction between what is best for the self and what is best for the relationship becomes blurred or disappears altogether. The trouble with applying the concept to women is that women are routinely taught that ignoring the self/relationship distinction is the path to self-fulfillment. In fact, the ability for a woman to ignore that distinction is regarded as a mark of her maturity.

There is a second way that fusion is an implicitly gendered concept. Fused people are described by Bowen as living "in a 'feeling' world," and spending the majority of their "life energy . . . maintaining the relationship system about them. . . . They are incapable of using the differentiated 'I' . . . in their relationship with others" (1966, p. 357). In this culture the foregoing statements comprise an adequate description of a so-called healthy woman (Broverman, Vogel, Broverman, Clarkson, and Rosenkrantz, 1972). Women are trained to be relational, to take care of the relational aspects of *all* our lives, to respond to the feelings of others, and specifically to avoid saying *I* want, *I* need. In contrast to fused people, differentiated people are "principle-oriented, goal-directed," "not affected by either praise or criticism from others," able to "assume total responsibility for self," and to "disengage from [intense emotional experiences] and proceed on a self-directed course at will" (Bowen, 1966, p. 359). Correctly acculturated men are trained in just such skills.

The fused/differentiated dichotomy is mistaken in polarizing human capacities. The mistake is compounded by reflecting the culture's higher valuation of autonomy skills over relational skills, i.e., the high valuation of manly skills over womanly skills. The effect is to polarize the sexes. Men, by their cultural training, will appear highly differentiated and thus will be labeled normal and healthy. Women, by their cultural training, will appear less differentiated and then be labeled pathological. We challenge the valuation that leads to such a result. This earth would be a safer, more habitable place if more than only the female half of the race were trained to nurture relationships, to respond to the feelings and opinions of others, and to foster the well-being of others.

The overlapping biases against women and relatedness inherent in Bowen's schema become even more apparent when the concept of fusion extends to describe what happens in intense emotional experiences. Bowen claims that even the well-differentiated person "relax[es] ego boundaries for the pleasurable sharing of 'selfs'," and then will need to disengage from this kind of "emotional fusion" to go on about (his) business (1966, p. 359). The disengagement counteracts the feeling of "too much togetherness, with its accompanying sense of loss of self. . . . " (Kerr, 1981, p. 236). This conceptualization of intimacy again represents the culture's view (which is men's view) that intimacy represents a danger—that it is life threatening rather than life giving, depleting rather than enhancing, and therefore best taken in small discrete doses. In contrast, women experience intimacy as enlarging, expanding, and defining the self, not obliterating it. Obliteration of signs of self may occur for women, but not because of the experience of intimacy *per se*.

Since the gender bias in this concept redoubles when viewing women in relationships with one another, we suggest that the therapist first consider alternative explanations for observed behavior in lesbian couples which they might otherwise describe as "fusion." For example:

(1) A relationship between a man and a woman in which she is always pulling for more and putting out more while he moves near and far, tolerating intimacy for only brief periods, is usually seen as normal and typical. If, however, the relationship is comprised of two women, both of whom are trained and ready to engage for a prolonged period in intense relating, then it may look pathological by comparison. Therapists should consider that they may be viewing richness rather than fusion.

(2) Lesbians have available to them a small community of kindred souls, surrounded by a society which is antipathetic or openly hostile to their existence. Thus the social context in which lesbians exist makes the penalties of losing a partner higher than would be the case with heterosexual clients. Rather than an inadequate sense of self, it may be this fear that causes the panic and desperate holding on that therapists often identify as evidence of fusion.

(3) Similarity, mirroring, or twinning, all phenomena which therapists have observed in lesbian couples, need not represent fusion, but rather a benign identification with each other, a protective response to a hostile surround.

(4) A therapist may be led to the diagnosis of fusion because of an unexamined envy of the observed closeness or because of an ambivalence about intimacy.

(5) The vocabulary and emotions women have been taught to associate with erotic attachment are laden with sacrifice and catastrophe. "Nothing matters to me but you." "I cannot live without you." When a woman describes herself to a man this way, the words sound normal and familiar. When a woman describes herself to a woman this way, the words signal fusion. Recognize this reaction as homophobic.

(6) A woman may be suffering from the consequences of a cognitive error which has given her to believe that she by herself is

inadequate to meet the demands of her life. This cognitive error is common in women as it is taught to them at an early age. It results in excessive dependency on a partner who is erroneously seen as having all the qualities that the woman herself lacks. The emotional component of this cognitive error is the panic the woman feels at any threat of the loss of such a profoundly important relationship, a reaction often exacerbated in lesbian relationships because of the conditions cited above, i.e., limited choices, increased intimacy, and heightened identification. Still, this reaction is neither clarified nor adequately described by calling it fusion.

Boundary. Boundary is the "line" around a set of people formed by the rules governing membership and participation inside that set. The term facilitates discussion in family therapy about the responsibilities and privileges of one group in relation to another, one part of the family in relation to another, and even one individual in relation to another. Whatever the original intent for the term, it has come to be commonly used in a way that moves it from making neutral distinctions—yours versus theirs—to being a philosophy of life: "Keep your boundaries clear." Whether said eloquently by theoreticians or instructively to clients, the emphasis is on ownership, possessiveness, protectiveness, separation, caution, and vigilance. Much more is written on what must be kept out than what must be let in; more on clarity and firmness than on fluidity and adaptability; more on what ought to be than on what might suit. Little is mentioned in the family therapy literature about ever loosening the grip on boundary, about times when it would be advantageous to lower the guard such as in play, crises, transitions, and certain groupings. As we began our work with the women reported in this chapter, we found that family therapy theory provided no direction telling us we should examine the necessities and benefits that would lead some couples, in this case lesbian couples, to avoid the tight boundary typically recommended. As a result, early in therapy, the women looked in error or in trouble, even though other boundaries in their lives (regarding work and families of origin) seemed to function well.

We want to challenge the use of boundary as a prescriptive rather than descriptive term. Other than the incest taboo, the key purpose of prescribing boundaries appears to be to protect hierarchies in the family, which are also prescribed. Such a vision of family is in the service of patriarchy and its favored mode, domination. Other ways of managing family life are seldom explored in family therapy.

The emphasis on boundary indicates that family therapy views relationships in the family, and relationships in general, as battles for territory, as power struggles from first to last. Undoubtedly there are people who experience relationships in precisely that way, but there are other ways to experience relationships. It is unnecessarily restrictive on the field to create no other metaphors and attend to no other models. Lesbian couples do intend a different vision: relationships based not on power politics, but on intimacy, mutuality, interdependence, and equality.

Treatment

Goals

Our goals with the group in treatment were:

(1) To help each woman identify her individual needs.
(2) To explore with each woman what it would mean for her to take care of her individual needs and the consequences that might flow from doing so.
(3) To normalize conflict, increase tolerance for it, and expand resources for resolving it.
(4) To encourage the women to negotiate explicit rules regarding the patterns of interaction that would suit them, especially with respect to defining the nature of primary relationships and the expectations about tasks, money, sex, and closeness.
(5) To support the women in their reliance on the resources available in the lesbian community.

Plan

Individual needs. An important way of helping the women recognize their needs is to identify something in what they are already saying and doing as an expression of an individual need. The expression may be described to them as overstated, understated, or disguised, but it will help validate direct expression if the therapists indicate that there is already *some* expression and show them that some expression is unavoidable. The therapists can request a direct statement of the identified need and work with the speaker's own reactions to making the statement more direct.

Consequences of needs. Once some progress has been made in recognizing and stating individual needs, each woman will require assistance in reacting to the consequences of those needs on others. The therapists will help each woman articulate the consequences for herself, and coach the owner of the need to hear the discussion without invalidating her need, even if it has undesired consequences for others.

Conflict. Options for dealing with conflict can be expanded for the women by interrupting their efforts to palliate and by encouraging them to relate to each other as competent adult women. The therapists can explain to them that when they are indirect and nonconfrontive, they infantilize each other and deprive one another of opportunities to demonstrate maturity and strength. By making explicit any implicit conflict in the group, the therapists can invite the women to talk through the issue during the therapy session and can act as coach for each participant while the other group members observe. Instructions can be given on fair fighting techniques, such as using "I" statements, staying with single issues, and putting a time limit on the argument.

Explicit expectations. This goal requires that the women learn about their expectations in primary relationships and what each is inferring about the other's expectations. Thus it is related to the first goal of recognizing individual needs. Differing expectations between partners can then be discussed and negotiated with the help of the therapists and the support of friends.

Resources. To legitimate the importance which the lesbian community plays as a resource in these women's lives, the therapists can acknowledge the friendship network, dinner club, women-centered musical events, and political activities which comprise the community that supports and nurtures lesbian women.

Kathy, Kim, Rita, Ruth

During the next few months, we encouraged Ruth to express her grief and anger regarding the loss of Rita as her lover both to Rita and to the group. Gradually Ruth became more settled about the change in her relationship with Rita, and started developing a new relationship. As is not unusual in the lesbian community, the other women in the group warmly included Ruth's new lover in their dinners and outings. This move seemed to take care of Ruth's desire to stay connected not only to Rita but to Kim and Kathy. Soon, Ruth decided that she no longer needed the sessions because she had completed what she needed to with Rita and trusted that her friendship with Rita and with the other members would continue. We concurred with Ruth's assessment.

Kathy's display of empathy in every session was remarkable. She always sat near the one who was in the most pain. She wept as they told their stories, reached out to comfort them physically, and held her own story inside so as not to take attention away from the one she believed needed it most. We challenged Kathy that she was interfering with the development of a mutual and reciprocal empathy among the group members by not giving the others a chance to nurture her. We suggested to the others that whenever Kathy offered expressions of concern to them, they might ask her if she could be holding back a need for some attention. After this suggestion, group members began to watch for behaviors on the part of any of them that might mask individual need and to comment on the advantages of direct over indirect requests.

Kathy demonstrated confusion about whether she would prefer a primary relationship with Rita or Kim, weeping over the potential loss of either of them. We asked her to define her needs and to tell us how each woman seemed to fulfill them. Kathy's response led us to believe that the question of her own needs in a relationship had never occurred to her; she had believed that the only legitimate question was who needed her.

After a few thoughtful moments, she acknowledged that Rita's energy and enthusiasm fulfilled her sexually and emotionally. When she began to speak about Kim, it seemed to us that her awareness and her words were formed at the same time. She said that Kim fulfilled her need for shared history, security, and familiarity, all represented in the home they had created together and in her inclusion in Kim's loving family—a family quite different from her abusive alcoholic parents, both of whom were now dead. Our understanding of this response was that Kim had given Kathy her first real home; its value must surely have been increased by the sanctuary it provided from the hostile world. The thought of losing it terrified Kathy. This interpretation seemed to fit as she went on in tears describing their shared life of fifteen years.

Rita displayed an exaggerated selflessness in her unconditional regard for Kathy. She repeatedly stated that she would support Kathy in whatever decision she might come to, even though she thoroughly enjoyed their sexual and emotional intimacy and hoped it would continue. We suggested to Rita that she might be denying to herself how important Kathy had become. When we asked Rita how she was taking care of her own needs, she said that she spent as much time with Kathy as circumstances would allow while being prepared for Kathy to move back to Kim at any time. Given the extent of her attachment, we warned Rita that she might be overestimating her ability to accept whatever happened and encouraged her to speak up as her reactions surfaced during the course of the therapy. She promised to do so.

Throughout these months Kim stayed firm in her desire to have Kathy move back to their house and try again to have a primary, sexually exclusive relationship. She expressed sadness that Kathy did not share in her resolve, but she hoped that when she returned from her long-planned trip to Europe over the summer, Kathy would be ready to move back with her. We asked Kim what would motivate Kathy to make the move. She replied that the desire to be a couple again would motivate Kathy to try. When we pressed further, Kim admitted that all their attempts at being sexually intimate in the last year had been unsatisfying for both of them but believed that time and the elimination of distractions might make for better success.

We asked if Kathy and Rita's relationship acted as a complication. Kim said that her requests of Kathy to stop seeing Rita led to such pain for Kathy that she always withdrew them. We wanted to assist Kim in going beyond her typical backing-off point, but she told us that she had no energy to do so. Because of their unclear and indirect style of communication, Kathy and Kim had not confronted each other effectively. It seemed to us that they were again operating out of the belief that the other was not strong enough to hear the truth, that they were unentitled to sexual satisfaction, that their desire to redefine their relationship was, in some way, disloyal.

Here was a good opportunity for us to help the women find better ways to deal with conflict. We asked each woman to describe her optimum desire and helped the group negotiate the resulting list. After some discussion, all agreed that Kathy would move back to the house but continue to see Rita while Kim was vacationing, a complicated solution but one that seemed to satisfy everyone. We outlined the possible consequences and how any one of the women could be the loser: Kim after returning from vacation might find herself without Kathy; Rita might become more involved and then be less able to extricate herself; Kathy might develop a greater attachment to the house and neighborhood as well as to Rita, and so her choice might be even more painful to make.

While Kim was away, Kathy and Rita told us how enjoyable their days were and how difficult it would be to end their sexual connection once Kim returned. Rita said that Kathy seemed happier now that she was back in her home. With reluctance, Rita said she was coming to realize that she could not compete with the fifteen years of history, family, and home that Kim and Kathy had shared. Kathy again emphasized how essential her home and neighborhood were to her, and how much she did not want to lose Kim as a friend and soulmate. However, she also said that it was hard to think of her as a lover.

In the session several weeks later when Kim returned, Kathy announced that she had decided to live on her own somewhere in the old neighborhood and date Rita as well as others. With much prompting from us, Kim told Kathy that she was sad and disappointed, but she spoke with very little affect. Rita also tried to disguise her feelings, using again a display of total acceptance. We suggested to Rita that she seemed to want to portray for Kathy an idealized image of the all-giving lover, and that this image was to her own disservice. We encouraged her to honor whatever feelings might come and not conclude that doing so would be turning away from her friend. Rita agreed to try. Kathy explained that her decision to create her own home arose from her awareness of the importance a home held for her—the home rather than Kim, who had faded as a sexual partner long ago.

In the next session, we learned that despite the intentions expressed in the prior session, Kathy had not moved out of Kim's house and instead continued to live with her. When asked about how she intended to satisfy her affectional/sexual needs, Kathy said she was not going to address that dimension for fear that Kim would not allow her to live with her while dating other women. In this way she hoped to avoid conflict, at least until an actual situation necessitated it. When we asked Kim to clarify her own position, she stated that it was not acceptable for Kathy to live with her and be sexually involved elsewhere. She hoped that, through the experience of living together, Kathy would desire her again. We asked Kim how exactly she envisioned that this change might take place. When pressed, she admitted that she really could not imagine it.

We offered the observation that the solution Kathy and Kim had come to did not seem likely to last long and wondered if perhaps it was their way of postponing an inevitable loss. Since they agreed, we encouraged them to spend time exploring ways of making a life together to see if they could incorporate what each wanted. In making this suggestion, we were aware that it would not be an easy task. Our visions of what we want in a relationship are easily clouded by heterosexist assumptions which block other possibilities for structuring relationships. Despite the difficulty, we urged them to the task, explaining that failure to be explicit increases the risk of living lives driven by assumptions that do not really fit.

Two weeks later, Kathy reported that she was living in the house, Kim was living in the spare room of a friend's house, and Rita was moving into a smaller apartment. Kathy and Kim agreed that the house held more meaning for Kathy than for Kim, so Kathy would continue living there while they discussed the possibility of selling. The physical moves denoted a significant shift for Kathy and Kim in their view of the relationship. They told us that they had spent long evenings analyzing whether their relationship met their individual needs. Their conclusion was that it no longer could.

Once they had ceased their efforts to make the relationship "work," Kathy and Kim were able to talk about their long-standing sexual difficulties. Kim admitted that she had always been frightened by Kathy's sexual intensity. We suggested that the source of such fright may be the specter of losing the intimacy produced by the intensity, losing that other who has come even nearer. Kim acknowledged that possibility but said with some embarrassment that all she knew for certain was that sex held little importance for her. While stating that this issue did not need to be thoroughly examined in Kathy's and Rita's presence, we suggested to Kim that perhaps her own sexual interest might not be deficient in *any* sense, but just different from Kathy's. This perspective was an obvious comfort to Kim. Kathy acknowledged that she had eventually given up trying to get Kim interested in sex. We wondered aloud if this was simply an extension of their rule about conflict: "If you cannot get what you want from your partner, backing off is preferable to fighting about it." Both women agreed with our interpretation.

We pointed out to the three women that Rita had said nothing during the session, that it had never seemed germane for us to ask for her comments, and that neither Kathy nor Kim had had any requests of her. After they discussed their responses to our observation, they concluded that Kathy and Kim had some private business in therapy that was not relevant to Rita, Ruth, or anyone else. We then arranged a session for Kathy and Kim alone to ritualize the ending of their sexual relationship.

At the scheduled session, Kathy and Kim started by declaring their unwillingness to say good-bye. We reminded them that the influence of heterosexism would make good-bye seem necessary simply because they were ending their sexual relationship. They need not participate in that thinking, we noted. They said that in many ways they still felt as close to each other as they had when they were lovers even though sex was not desired. With some specific guidance from us, they began to grieve the loss of their sexual relationship, openly sharing the pain and sadness of their last years together. In time they moved into talking more about the importance of the relationship, both past and present, and insisted on having it for the future. We proposed that though not born of the same mother, they had found each other to be a good sister and were experiencing how precious and wonderful a sister could be. Kathy answered that in fact none of the women in the group had a sister and wondered if that was part of the reason that leaving each other was so painful. One of the therapists shared that she does have a sister and would also despair if she could not count on her for special times and long talks into the night for the rest of their lives.

Kim and Kathy seemed moved by the idea of looking on one another as sister and enjoyed the shape it gave their future. Then they became worried that since they were not biological sisters, outsiders might not understand or support the continuing desire of each to keep the other so central to her life. Kim said she had already experienced trouble, explaining that the women she had recently dated felt threatened and distrustful of her relationship with Kathy despite her telling them it was nonsexual. We sympathized with this problem and said that even with the biological tie to our own sisters, there was often trouble, our husbands and lovers having been jealous of the bond. In the lesbian community, we noted, the problem would obviously be more complicated. Since the community is so small and the risk of exposing one's self to a stranger is so high, women do tend to date their friends and the line between friend and lover is frequently crossed. We urged them over the next week to think of other difficulties they could envision. They suggested including Rita in the assignment and inviting her to come next time. We agreed.

All three women came to the next session. Each one described various difficulties envisioned for future relationships, and we noted that these difficulties had a common cause: ambiguity about expectations in relationships. Here was another version of the problem we had worked on throughout therapy. This time we phrased it as an ambiguity about commitment. In response, they started talking about the "oppression of marriage." We asked for specifics and they all spoke at once, completing each other's sentences as if they had discussed this topic many times. They spoke of the unequal power between husband and wife, the lack of mutuality in tasks and caregiving, and the requirement to find fulfillment of all needs within the marriage. We pointed out that these had to do with heterosexism, not with commitment itself. We asked, "If you were free to spread your commitment among as many as you wished, to whom would you be willing to commit for what?" With sudden ease and enjoyment, they described commitments of various attentions and services to several different friends and then moved to the threesome in the room. Kim and Kathy committed themselves to protecting their sisterhood and to continuing to learn about it; Kathy and Rita committed themselves to a period of sexual exclusivity while they examined the potential between them; Kim and Rita committed themselves to a friendship marked by small amounts of time sharing music and conversation. At our suggestion, all three recognized that whatever was unstated was outside the commitment and open to experimentation and negotiation.

Six weeks later, Rita, Kim, and Kathy came to the session. All three reported that they had resolved the issues that had brought them to therapy. Rita was enjoying school and her relationship with Kathy. Kathy was enjoying her house, time with Rita, and her evolving relationship with Kim. Kim was enjoying dating and her evolving relationship with Kathy. They all periodically had dinner with Ruth.

Pitfalls

These are the pitfalls that await the feminist family therapist in working with lesbian couples:

(1) *Insisting, "Some of my best friends are lesbians."* The central pitfall for the family therapist working with lesbian clients is failure to recognize mutually shared homophobia. The fact that therapist and client seem to espouse the same values may simply reflect their common rearing in a culture with a long history of revulsion and fear of women who love women. Despite all efforts to be rid of prejudice, the therapist needs to stay keenly aware of the remaining homophobic and heterosexist bias or it will surely insinuate itself into the therapy.

(2) *Holding onto a hands-off policy.* Out of her desire to respect the uniqueness of her lesbian clients' experience, the therapist may be reluctant to address issues which she would not hesitate to comment on if she were working with a heterosexual couple. While it is sometimes wise for therapists to assume an anthropological stance with clients who present unfamiliar problems and situations, this stance can be held too long. The therapist is thereby deskilled and the clients will not be well-served.

(3) *Detecting only legends and visionaries.* Although most family theories ignore or implicitly pathologize lesbian experience, feminist family therapists may err in the opposite direction by idealizing lesbian existence. The lesbian may be viewed as heroic for having escaped the bonds of heterosexual coupling and rejecting the oppression of possessiveness and inequality which are too often characteristic of heterosexual relationships. To the extent that therapists idealize any clients, they limit their ability to be useful.

(4) *Overestimating identification, underestimating difference.* The therapist may believe that sharing womanhood with her lesbian clients is so fundamental a similarity as to render insignificant any dissimilarity arising from the lesbian experience. Although this error is most frequently made in the interest of establishing empathy with the clients, it is inevitably a disservice because it results in failure to appreciate the uniqueness of the clients' own life. A related pitfall for therapists is to mistake their familiarity with feminist thought for an understanding of lesbian experience. Actually, much feminist writing does not address lesbian experience at all.

(5) *Assuming that if you've seen one, you've seen them all.* In spite of a commitment not to see lesbianism as a form of pathology, the feminist family therapist may fall into the trap of classifying these clients by their sexual orientation rather than by the way they present themselves in therapy. Such an error will lead to the absurd conclusion that all lesbians are alike and have the same problems.

IX
THE ABUSIVE RELATIONSHIP

So taunt me
And hurt me
Deceive me
Desert me
I'm yours 'til I die
So in love
So in love
So in love with you, my love,
Am I.

— *Kate in Cole Porter's "Kiss Me Kate"*

IT WAS HER FIRST SESSION. With hands and voice trembling, Angie described her troubles to me. She was chronically unable to sleep, concentrate, mother, or work. She had been diagnosed as having a spastic colon. All her energy was being absorbed by her struggles with Hank, from whom she had been divorced for two years. Divorce, however, had failed to separate them, and they were living together again.

She told of Hank's betrayals—promising to quit the other woman in his life, and then continuing to see her. She told of Hank's reversals—telling her in one breath how to behave so as not to ruin their chances to "make it" and then denying that he had ever held out hope to her. She told of Hank's rages—reaching unexpectedly to pull the children's hair or push her against the wall. She told of Hank's harassments—phoning her at her office ten or twelve times a day, shouting insults at regular intervals, waking her in the night "to get one more thing straight," threatening a custody battle. Still, she said, it was only with him that she "felt secure." With certainty born of hope, she believed that deep down he really loved her and that her own love for him would bring out the goodness in him. These ties bound her to the relationship and made her want to keep it.

Given this description, many therapists are drawn irresistibly to diagnose Angie as masochistic, a term that has a long and esteemed history in psychology (Deutsch, 1944; Freud, 1924/1959; Roazen, 1985; Stolorow, 1975; see also Caplan, 1985). As a diagnosis, masochism is almost exclusively reserved for women, and is meant to describe a mentally disordered person who not only persistently consents to her own harm and abuse in a relationship, but also appears to derive some pleasure out of that pain. The notion that she is actually motivated by the "sweetness of suffering" distinguishes the masochistic woman from other women who also suffer, such as the poor woman who struggles daily for survival (Shainess, 1984). The masochist wants to be dominated by a man and derives all her self-esteem from his approval.

From a systems perspective, the "masochistic" woman is best understood in the context of her relationship with a "sadistic" partner. In this context the words "masochism" and "sadism" are used in their broadest sense, to describe a pervasive attitude toward one's primary relationship, not to denote preferences of sexual pleasure. The gratification of the sadistic man complements the purported gratification of the masochistic woman. He feels justified in causing her psychological (and sometimes physical) pain on the grounds that he is giving her what she truly wants and needs— domination by a *real* man. This rationalization is so potent that the sadistic man seldom presents himself for psychotherapy. He feels no conflict about his role since her devotion to him, despite her pain, is proof that he is accomplishing his task.

In the case described here the abusive man refused to be involved in therapy and professed to feel no guilt or even doubt about his role in the relationship. Thus on the most literal level this case was one of individual therapy. We believe, however, that understanding Angie required careful attention to the context in which her problem occurred. Hank loomed large in that context.

As feminists, we challenged the conceptualization of Angie as masochistic because her behavior was merely the fulfillment of cultural expectations for women, not an example of deviance[1]. We did not need to rely on an individual woman's psychological constructs to explain behavior which appears to be self-hating; we can point to a culture which contains many woman-hating requirements such as borderline malnourishment to achieve the culture's definition of feminine beauty, work which is compensated at less than two-thirds the rate of a man's, and a needy, subservient stance for women in their relationships with men. Indeed, it is because of this prescribed stance towards men that the other requirements exist and have the force they do. For a woman to comply with such requirements necessarily involves her in behavior that appears to be self-hating, whatever her own motives and perceptions may be.

Angie

Angie was 31 years old, divorced, and the mother of two young children. She was employed as a low-level manager in a large service-oriented company. She and Hank met as high school students, dated for several years, then married after college. Angie described Hank as very handsome, strong-willed, and volatile. Originally attracted to him because he always seemed to know what he wanted, she had come to see his certainty as stubbornness. The marriage became increasingly conflictual, at times escalating to physical violence. Although Angie never stopped feeling great love and intense attraction for her husband, she became involved in an extramarital relationship. After several months, she divorced her husband, planning to marry her more gentle and even-tempered lover.

Divorce, however, was not sufficient to loosen Angie's connection with Hank. Angie remained involved with him on a sexual as well as emotional level. After breaking off with her lover, she dated several other men, but said that she never really loved any man but Hank and wanted to re-marry him.

For his part, Hank was involved with another relationship, but

[1]Similarly, Hank's sadistic behavior was an enlargement of the culturally prescribed and culturally enforced role for men, better known as macho. Our purpose in this chapter will be to explicate the woman's psychological and social context. For an explication of men's context, see Ehrenreich (1983) and Miller (1976).

vigorously pursued the relationship with Angie, telling her that he also wanted to re-marry her. After eight months of divorce, he and Angie began living together again, although Angie knew he intended to continue seeing the other woman. When Angie complained, Hank accused her of putting too much pressure on him to make a decision about their relationship.

It was at this point that Angie came to see me. She wanted to be with Hank, but was having trouble sleeping, working, caring for her children, and living up to his expectations of her. She asked me to help her stop being so selfish and impatient. She wanted to stop reacting to his angry tantrums and stop crying about "his sleeping with me one night and going out on me the next." Hank told her that, if he and Angie were ever to have a chance, these conditions were an inevitable and unharmful part of their lives at the moment and had to be endured until they "played out." Angie's aim was to learn to endure. Her reward would be marriage to the man she loved, and she fervently believed that he would come to "the hidden best of himself" by way of her love.

Angie's acute distress was interfering with her daily functioning; I addressed this first. Lowering her anxiety began with her engagement in the therapeutic relationship itself. The experience of being listened to, attended to, and supported was a unique one for Angie. The fact that she had a particular time and person for her alone reduced the sense of isolation that fans panic. When I reflected back to her what she had told me and asked for clarifications, Angie seemed comforted by the knowledge of having taken the first in a series of steps to lead herself out of the maze of misery she presented. To extend this sense of comfort beyond the therapy hour and into the week, I asked Angie to engage in some specific techniques for managing stress. She agreed.

Although Angie's request of therapy was assistance in tolerating Hank's behavior, I found myself replacing that goal with my own: to teach Angie to interact with Hank in a way that showed more self-respect. I thought about the problem in these terms: Why would a woman, with other financial options, stay emotionally connected to a man she has legally divorced when even she describes the relationship, past and present, as unsatisfactory in fundamental ways? Why does such a woman remain in a psychologically abusive relationship? If she valued herself more highly, she would not tolerate Hank's abuse. If she could not stop the abuse, she would leave the relationship with finality. I concluded that only a woman who placed little value on her own well-being would stay. This way of thinking led to an impasse in therapy.

My efforts to encourage Angie to develop more self-respectful action focused not only on her relationship with Hank but also on other areas. I helped Angie to pursue friendships and activities with her children as well as identify other interests. As for the relationship with Hank, I began by rehearsing with her how to confront Hank directly about his abusiveness. After several unsuccessful attempts to convince Angie to move these rehearsals to real life, I shifted to less confrontational methods. I suggested that when Hank shouted insults, Angie should turn on the tape recorder, telling him she needed to bring me an accurate description of his opinion of her. When he called at the office, she should allow the conversation to last one minute, then have him hold the line while she attended to some office matters, then return to the conversation for one minute, put him on hold again, and so on. She did not follow these suggestions.

Confused and frustrated by the failure of my approach, I examined the knot of questions binding me: If Angie will take steps neither to stop the abuse nor to leave, what am I supposed to do for her? Why is she so scared to act? Why is she wasting her time, her life, on this man? How can I pull her out? Rather than being calmly analytical, these questions felt charged with pain and anger. Struck by my strong reactions to Angie, I took the case to my consultation group.

Consultation

In the first several therapy sessions, the therapist made suggestions to Angie about how to behave with Hank in a manner that would denote greater self-respect and less tolerance for his abusiveness. The relationship between Angie and the therapist seemed warm and collaborative. Angie liked her suggestions and felt better about herself when thinking she might have options in dealing with Hank, yet she had not followed through on a single one. Every time it appeared that Angie was seeing the light the therapist held out, she came back with something that cancelled what she had previously said, apparently concluding that love held out a brighter, warmer light. We also discovered in consultation that the therapist was experiencing a strong identification with Angie, for Angie evoked recollections of the therapist's own past relationships with men, ones in which she herself had stayed too long, worked too hard, and tolerated too much.

We could easily validate the therapist's identification with Angie as well as the frustration born of her hopes for Angie. As a group of feminist family therapists who share the vision of egalitarian relationships, we soon recognized the source of the strong reaction to Angie: Angie is a painful reminder to us all of the widely expected — and nonegalitarian — role for women in their relationships with men. Moreover, Angie has been taught — as we and most women have been — to place her energy, worth, and power in the service of making a relationship work.

In this initial phase of the consultation, we decided to have one member of the team join the therapist for an interview with Angie. The intent of therapy remained the same: to free Angie from the stranglehold of the relationship with Hank. We did suggest a change in approach, proposing that the consultant use a paradoxical strategy of taking Angie's assumptions to the extreme in an exaggerated, but supportive, prescription of her current behavior. We hoped Angie would then push against that version of her life and thus move herself out of her current position.

Consultant / Therapist / Client

During the interview, the consultant began this new approach by gently chiding the therapist for her assumption that happiness is a universal goal. After talking with Angie about her background, the consultant was able to develop evidence for her speculation that among women in Angie's family, ethnic group, and religion, the values of loyalty, patience, and commitment in the face of suffering far outweigh the value of happiness. The consultant cited many of Angie's interactions with Hank to support the idea that this view of life was the guiding influence for Angie. Angie found the interpretation hard to argue against in the face of her own behavior, yet she clung tenaciously to her assertion that the preeminent goal in her life was to be happy, and that the best chance for that happiness was with Hank. The consultant expressed sympathy for Angie's desire for happiness, but reiterated the position that, if faced with a choice, Angie would opt for loyalty and service rather than happiness. She instructed Angie to teach the therapist more about these values, especially about the importance of living them out with Hank.

As the interview ended, Angie pushed against the framework we had created, entreating her therapist to keep up the good work of making suggestions about dealing with Hank differently. She emphasized that she was *not* staying in the relationship to gratify the hypothesized desire to live a life of virtuous struggle and forbearance. Rather, she stated that she deeply loved Hank and believed that through the triumph of her love he could become the fine person she knew lurked beneath his volatile, angry exterior. She also asked the therapist to keep giving her direction on how to participate more effectively in other parts of her life, those parts lived outside the relationship with Hank.

Consultation

In spite of what appeared to be initial success with this new approach, all of us—the consultants as well as the therapist—realized that we could not maintain this strategy. We could not create a paradoxical position exaggerated enough to outdo the absurdity of society's actual position.[2] The attempt to do so leads the therapist into being a spokeswoman for society, urging the very principles and actions that she deplores. Paradoxical prescriptions, to avoid being unethical and punitive, must be palatable to the therapist whether they are followed or fought. Obviously such was not the case for us. The paradoxical strategy, though successful, was a betrayal not only of the therapist's own principles, but a betrayal of what Angie could come to believe about herself.

We also began to question our direction with Angie. All our

---

[2]The popular women's tee shirt logo "Whip me. Beat me. Write me bad checks" exemplifies the pervasive attitude that women are supposed to find submission an erotic experience.

thinking had been on how to free her from her relationship with Hank as well as from all the assumptions that held her there. In our commitment to help Angie see that the trouble begins with society's expectations, we wondered if we lost sight of her, her initial request, and our additional commitment to support the various ways of being a woman today. We decided our missionary zeal had overtaken our wisdom.

In looking for a new start, first we examined our current way of viewing Angie. We were seeing her as a trapped victim, and so we could only be rescuers to her. As an alternative, the addiction model came to mind. With it, she would still be seen as victim, but not such a passive one. This model might provide new kinds of leverage for us and for her.

Using the addiction model would have us see Angie as a woman who found herself compulsively dependent upon that which was destructive for her. It would have us see that she may dislike herself for the addiction, but could give it up with no more ease than an alcoholic, who is also the child of an alcoholic, could give up alcohol. After some discussion, we rejected that framework because it implied a long and necessary wait for Angie to "hit bottom" before any help could come. Women can become so caught up in the kind of struggle described by Angie that they are too depressed to get up in the morning, and may even commit suicide. Moreover, the addiction model only speaks to the obsessional aspect of Angie's problem, with no attention to her strengths. There is something we wanted to say about Angie's persistence, but calling it an addiction was not the direction we wished to follow.

We did not want to take a direction that would foreclose on the chance of finding some positive aspects of Angie's behavior, so that we could see Angie as exercising some strengths. We returned to focus on Angie's continual persistence. We began to develop the framework that Angie is the kind of person who needs to live "on the edge." Like a sky-diver who is energized by the ability to survive against all odds, Angie feels her strength when it is most fully tested — and she survives the test. The most familiar, creative, and validated test for her is surviving a difficult relationship.

Relieved that we had found a more respectful way to view Angie, we then began to challenge it: Is a difficult relationship a worthy place for a woman to put her strength? It is a familiar awareness that women's primary task in this society is to be relational, to maintain relationships, exactly to endure and persevere.[3] While men are taught to pursue a career, women are taught to become more and more proficient at caring for others, anticipating and satisfying their needs. For a man, the harder and more complicated the job, the greater the challenge. Do we believe persevering in a difficult relationship is just as worthy a struggle as persevering in a laboratory to find the cure for some dreaded disease? Each may come to no success, but does each receive equal honor for the effort manifest, the loyalty displayed, and the strength invested? Certainly the answer is no if one looks at the response of society; the man will be commended, the woman condemned, despite the fact that she has done exactly what society told her to do.

The bitter irony of gender role socialization is that boys and girls are excited by their respective pursuits, but while the man will be rewarded handsomely by society, the woman will be diagnosed masochistic. Even therapists typically let men get away with following gender-specific teachings, but once a woman walks into the office with emotional and somatic complaints, she is blamed for being foolish enough to take her concerns so much to heart. We examined the blame at the core of the early approaches we ourselves had taken with Angie. That blame was given in the hope that we could move away from the thin line that actually separates us from Angie. We saw ourselves in her; we were raised in the same schools.

We also reminded ourselves of our differences from Angie. What struck us most strongly was that we each had a variety of influences that helped us establish a positive identification as women which was more empowering than Angie's. Perhaps even more importantly, we currently had one another for professional and personal consultation and support, an invaluable resource which had no counterpart in Angie's life. We knew it to be of utmost importance to find ways in therapy to make such influences and experiences available to Angie. Before we proceeded to plan a

---

[3]This notion of woman enduring her difficult relationship with her man has been part of the popular culture for quite some time in song lyrics. A recent example is Tammy Wynette's omnipresent voice urging, "Stand By Your Man."

course for treatment, however, we needed to explore more fully the details and implications of the analysis we had begun.

Analysis

Consider what the psychologically abusive relationship for a woman feels like for her. Typically, she experiences a relationship with a man as necessary for her survival. With so much at stake, she finds herself easy prey to intimidation. She gives her needs a very low priority, and so does her partner. The one need she does acknowledge is to satisfy him. Unfortunately, even this need is continually thwarted. Never quite good enough or quick enough, she regularly encounters his haranguing temper and judges herself as a just target for his rage and disdain.

What was Angie doing in such a relationship? Was she merely acting out a *personal* problem of low self-esteem? On the contrary, Angie had completely absorbed the *societal* assumption about women that life itself, let alone self-esteem, requires a relationship with a man. Therefore, she would go to virtually any length to maintain it. Angie's unsuspecting and absolute adoption of this assumption had a woefully ironic result: she participated in her own victimization. The tolerance, patience, loyalty, and commitment that she worked so hard to manifest in order to maintain that crucial relationship were the very elements that allowed Hank's abuse to continue. Even worse, she remained unaware of the source of her suffering. She thought that the trouble came from her own inadequacies: she was not good enough. She did not call into question the basic assumption holding her in place. She had nowhere to stand that would give her the perspective to view it *as* an assumption. Following it as a truth brought the self-deprecation and pain that led her to therapy.

What compounded the problem was that Angie not only defined herself as worthwhile relative to her ability to maintain a relationship with this man, but also that she held herself exclusively accountable for the success or failure of the relationship. With the relationship structured in this one-sided manner, Angie stood alone, saving it by endurance, perseverance, and ultimate responsibility. Any slight change in the relationship was to her credit alone. If there were no perceivable changes, she could try harder with the knowledge that she was engaged in the only truly worthy pursuit: being in a relationship with her man and doing whatever had to be done to maintain it.

Such feelings and behavior on Angie's part reflected only a slight exaggeration of what women are routinely taught about the importance of relationships with men. This society has systematically trained women to see themselves as incapable of a life of autonomy and independence. For a woman to be without a man is, by all standard social definitions, to be incomplete. In such a society, it is not abnormal for a woman such as Angie to feel a desperate need for the help and approval of a man and to use great stores of perseverance, tolerance, and endurance to keep that man at her side. Yet when women carry out the cultural prescriptions of dependence on men, they are often labeled masochistic.

A fairly recent twist on the old label is to charge women like Angie with collusion. A family therapist for example might say that there is an obvious circularity in Angie's situation. Hank's aggressive behavior intimidated Angie into passive behavior; at the same time, Angie's passive behavior allowed Hank's aggressive behavior to continue. The more she endured, the more he created for her to endure; the more he created, the more she had to endure. As many writers would put it, Hank and Angie were producing this dance together.

This reasoning overlooks the major point: Angie and Hank were not involved in an intimate two-step, but rather in an intricate choreography that is culture-wide. Women in this culture have their assigned set of steps and men have theirs. Although the steps fit together, the female dancers are the ones who consistently view themselves as ultimately responsible for the success or failure of the dance, and perform it as if their lives depended on it. To expect an individual woman on her own to change her part significantly is to ignore the power of socially constructed and socially legitimated reality.

Earlier we noted that Angie's acceptance of societal assumptions led her to participate in her own victimization. To describe her as *colluding* with Hank, however, connotes a level of personal gain and perversity that is off the mark when applied to so large-scale an arrangement as we have been discussing. Appreciation of the societal context that sustains relationships like Angie's and Hank's dispels the notion of collusion and forces us to consider the cultural realities which restrict a woman's range of movement in situations like this.

First, challenging psychological abuse forcefully and decisively is not an option that would ever present itself to many women. In our culture, women are taught not to show power directly, not to use their strengths and influence on their own behalf. Indeed, women are typically afraid of being thought of as powerful. Jean Baker Miller says of women: "To act out of one's own interest and motivation is experienced as the psychic equivalent of being a destructively aggressive person. This is a self-image which few women can bear" (1982, p. 4). In fact, women may pay a high price if they show evidence of being powerful; their nonstereotypical stance is likely to leave them isolated from men and from other women. Several authors have traced the sources and consequences of this fear of women's power (Chernin, 1981; Dinnerstein, 1977; Miller, 1982; Orbach, 1978), but the point here is that acting with power for one's own sake is not a well-practiced or sought after skill for many women. This is one of the cultural facts that limits women's repertoire of available responses to abuse from a significant man.

Second, the customary and comfortable way for a woman to use her power is in the service of others—to foster their growth, supply their needs, aid their projects, support *their* power. Women know the value of their enabling role and do gain a sense of power and fulfillment from performing it. The most common, legitimate, and accessible way for a women to do so has been in a primary relationship with a man. In fact, enabling a man to do what he does in the world is the main way women have had to participate in the world themselves.

Rather than describe Angie as a masochist seeking suffering, we would suggest that she is seeking power—power in the primary way society sees as legitimate for women: standing by her man. Angie's belief that her love and patience can bring out the best in Hank is evidence that she senses her behavior as a powerful act, not a miserable act. The more she can stay with a difficult relationship, the more opportunity she provides herself for experiencing power. In this society, it is difficult for women to find anything comparable to the unqualified ratification bestowed upon them for being successful with a man.

Third, the alternatives for a woman in a situation like Angie's have considerable drawbacks. Women do have fewer economic and vocational opportunities than do men. Discrepancies in salaries, benefits, and recognition are real and restrictive. Moreover, the world is not a safe place for women. A primary benefit to having a man is the protection he provides against other men. Women are not foolish for considering all these facts.

There are apparent contradictions in our analysis. We say that Angie is not deviant and pathological, but we also come close to saying that in this culture a normal woman is a crazy person. We say that Angie was suffering from the abusive situation, but we also say that she gained power and fulfillment from staying in it. We say that we hope therapy will promote self-respect and self-awareness, but we also say that the culture has convinced her that self only has meaning in continuing self-destructive behavior in the service of her relationship.

These contradictions are unavoidable, for they derive from the real contradictions inherent in women's position today. There is some room for therapeutic movement even so. Although Angie might not be able to find or wait for a relationship with a man in which there is reciprocal nurturing and respect, she could be helped to make accommodations in the relationship that are less harmful to herself and to foster the well-being of neglected aspects of her life.

Treatment

Goals

The issue, then, is not about masochism or deviancy, but rather how to define normality. If Angie continued to look at herself and her life only through the lens that she had been taught to use, she could not make any choice except the one she had already made. Given a new way of viewing herself, however, she could make better choices.

Our goals for Angie's therapy were:

(1) For Angie to choose to continue or discontinue her relationship with Hank based on full awareness of her options both inside and outside the relationship.

(2) For Angie to continue to grow in competence as an employee, mother, friend, lover, and daughter.

Plan

Self-determination. For Angie to make an informed choice about her relationship required that she:

(1) come to know herself as a chooser, as one who has the right and the ability to make choices for herself;

(2) examine her options within the relationship;

(3) envision options outside the relationship as potentially meaningful.

As a preliminary step to seeing herself as someone with the ability to choose, Angie had to tell her story: how she came to believe what she did about herself, men, women, relationships, and life. The therapist's role would be to assist her by asking questions, thereby indicating to her that her beliefs are not self-evident truths and that the possibility of other beliefs exists. Once Angie could be jarred into this realization, she and the therapist could look more closely at specific beliefs Angie had heretofore not reflected upon. Especially important would be an examination of what she has been taught about women and men and how they are expected to lead their lives in this culture.

By moving the focus back and forth from public to personal, Angie could be helped to understand how her own unique and particular history served as a context for her adoption of cultural norms. Angie's memories and assumptions could serve as important sources for her and could be enriched by requesting that she consult the members of her family. How do the various members of her family feel about the course of their lives? Do they experience their lives as a product of their own choices?

As Angie is led to make a connection between her family's decisions and her own, she will gradually learn to discriminate between decisions she has made to fit her own needs and those that were automatic responses to what was expected. Making a similar discrimination about decisions of family members will further extend Angie's ability to evaluate. She can begin to conceive of choice and to explore her own personal wants, desires, aspirations, and dreams.

To assist Angie in examining the options available to her in the relationship with Hank, the therapist could ask her to articulate in behavioral terms current problems in the relationship. In addressing these problems, reframing and behavioral assignments would be aimed at helping Angie experience herself as active rather than passive. After her careful observation of the results of her new behaviors, Angie could gather information concerning the likelihood of any desired changes in her relationship with Hank. At the time of this assessment, Angie will need to clarify and perhaps expand what she views as legitimate expectations for a relationship. Discussion about her parents' marriage, comparisons of her experience in relationships with other men and women, and conversations with women friends about their relationships will facilitate this process.

Competence. In order for Angie to see options outside the relationship with Hank as important sources of meaning for her, she will have to explore her level of satisfaction with other relationships already present in her life. She is a mother, a daughter, a friend, and an employee. Does she know her strengths in these roles? Is she aware of how she feels about herself within these relationships? Can any of those relationships be enhanced in a way that would give her greater satisfaction?

The therapist will serve as a significant resource for Angie in discussing assumptions about motherhood and suggesting experiments with different ways of parenting. The therapist can also assist Angie in her relationship with her employer and supervisor by helping her learn to be more effective in making her opinions and needs clear to her co-workers. On the basis of her experience in the contexts available to her, she will be asked to reflect on differences in the way she feels about herself in the presence of various people. Extending the depth or breadth of her relationships can give Angie a fuller arena in which to explore herself. Clarifying her hopes for those relationships will add to her sense of herself as someone with more facets than can be stimulated by the one single focus she has had.

Angie

Following the consultation session, I found progress with Angie to be slow and unsteady, even though my purpose with Angie was clearer and more manageable. Her focus remained primarily on Hank, so our work to help her discover the cultural and familial sources of her learnings about womanhood needed to be directly tied to that focus rather than follow a coherent direction of its own. Perhaps the most telling exploration for her was spurred by our work on choice. I asked her to talk with her mother, and the results surprised her. Her mother said that she herself had *chosen* subservience as her way of *managing* her husband, a plan that had worked well, according to her, in spite of the costs. "But Hank is very different from your father in the way he is acting. You don't have to lie down and take those shenanigans of his—especially since you have a job!" It had not occurred to Angie that a cost/benefit analysis, let alone financial self-support, were relevant factors in designing action. In fact, the idea that her mother had acted with such intentionality was shocking. "I just thought that what I saw was the way mother *was*."

These talks with her mother grew out of Angie's efforts to put into concrete terms her current problems with Hank. She came to realize that she could not sort these out while she lived in his house and he dated other women. After several sessions spent discussing this issue, she and the children moved out of Hank's house. Soon after, another woman moved in with Hank, but neither of these changes lessened Hank's harassments or the intensity of his involvement with Angie.

As before, weeks were spent conferring with Angie on various strategies for dealing with these harassments, only to have her dismiss all suggestions as impossible to perform. Still, she seemed to delight in hearing the suggestions, so I continued them as a scenario for a future that could not yet be enacted. Consequently, Angie's reports of failures to carry them through did not elicit negative responses from me. Angie appeared surprised when she was not chastised or seen as incompetent. Gradually, she began to report experiments with setting some limits with Hank. For example, after four months Angie was able to hang up the phone when Hank called in the middle of the night, and several weeks later she was able to refuse calls from him at the office.

During occasional lulls in the action from Hank, Angie discussed her relationship with her children who, she believed, saw her as the "ultimate pushover." I gave suggestions about how to set and enforce reasonable limits with the children, and saw them briefly with Angie in therapy to discuss some new approaches to difficulties at bedtimes and mealtimes. These sessions proved useful as far as the children's behavior was concerned, but Angie had difficulty taking any credit for the change. She began to see me as the expert on her children, bringing more and more issues about child management into the therapy and asking me for more and more advice. To break this cycle, I replaced advice with explorations of Angie's assumptions about her ability and rights to care for the children. Further, I made certain that I found some aspect of Angie's own judgments and efforts to support. Eventually the complaints about her children ceased and Angie began to experience herself as a more competent mother.

With each small success, Angie seemed encouraged to make other changes as well. From time to time, she brought concerns to therapy about her supervisor who interspersed frequent sexual overtures with demands that Angie accomplish ten hours of work in an eight hour work day. I helped her to distinguish legitimate from illegitimate requests and to clarify for herself the terms of the contract constituting her relationship with her employer. In addition, I used the various incidents Angie reported from her office to point out the overlooked signs in them that she was a trusted and valued employee. After rehearsals with me, Angie was able to establish boundaries around her work time and her rights at the office.

Concurrent with the strides Angie was making in various areas of her life was her continuing struggle with Hank. It seemed to me that Angie and Hank were caught up in a particularly vicious circle. In the midst of the repetitions, Angie fought to behave in ways that would honor the changes she was making in her other relationships, but small successes were easily overshadowed by her sad and frightened awareness that it was the relationship with Hank which felt most important.

Eventually, perhaps motivated by the slight differences he perceived in Angie's behavior toward him, Hank ended the relationship with his latest girlfriend and declared his readiness to recommit himself to his relationship with Angie. To her own surprise, Angie was reluctant to give up her current life, which included a relationship with a man she had been seeing for several months. She also suspected that Hank might turn again to his girlfriends. She told Hank that they needed to have a therapy session together to confer on their best course. Hank agreed. He failed to keep the appointment however and soon backed out of the agreement for the conference altogether.

Angie decided that before her relationship with Hank could proceed, they needed to establish some ground rules. During the next two months of therapy, she developed a list of three prerequisites to a reconciliation with Hank. The very fact that Angie could see herself as active participant in defining the relationship was testimony to the significance of the changes she had made in therapy. Angie informed Hank that, before she would move in with him again, he would have to agree to (1) enter marital therapy with her; (2) assure her that there would be no more physical or verbal abuse; and (3) promise not to see other women. Angie wanted Hank to commit himself to these requirements for six months.

Hank was infuriated by Angie's new stance. He threatened, cajoled, and in other ways tried to persuade her that her requirements were unfair and unrealistic. Angie held firm. After several weeks, it became clear that neither of them was going to capitulate. For the first time in the history of their relationship, they began to disengage.

As of this writing, Angie is dating a man whom she describes as supportive, kind, and loving. Her competence and her recognition of it—at work and at home with her children—continue to grow. She enjoys her friends and has pursued some ventures on her own, a jazz class and a course in art history. Reportedly Hank is about to marry, a fact that gives Angie some sadness, but also some relief.

A key factor in Angie's therapy was the change in me. Through the discussions with the consulting group, I found a way to respect Angie's persistence, ideals, and forthrightness. That respect reached far enough to cause me to withdraw from the battle with Angie and allow her to focus on Hank as long as she needed. Angie borrowed that respect until it became her own. By doing so, she was able to enhance many aspects and relationships of her life. The value that she found in these ultimately became a counterweight that pulled her away from Hank.

Pitfalls

These are the pitfalls that await the feminist family therapist in addressing abusive relationships:

(1) *Saving her against her will.* The greatest mistake that a therapist can make with a client like Angie is to try to pry her out of a bad relationship "for her own good." Such a strategy indicates to the client that she is neither being heard nor accepted by the therapist. It places the therapist in the untenable position of validating the societal bias which tells Angie that she is not competent to make her own decisions or form her own judgments.

(2) *Underestimating the strength of the other.* Systemic thinking sometimes seems to imply that all persons in the system are equal in power, or that power differences do not matter, since the circuit is of interest. In the real world however, the client may well feel herself outranked and find the loud tantrums, physical threats, financial ploys, and flaunted infidelities of her partner to be frightening, maddening, and worthy of circumspect behavior on her part. If this experienced power differential is not taken seriously by the therapist, her assignments and goals will be perceived as ludicrous.

(3) *Seeing the client as a symbol.* A client like Angie—unassertive, forbearing, and downtrodden—is the perfect product of the culture which feminists are working very hard to change. Because she represents a type which feminists would like to see made obsolete, it may be especially difficult for the therapist to refrain from disdainful or patronizing remarks. The more nar-

row, incomplete, or recent her own escape from fitting the cultural stereotype of woman, the greater the danger of a self-congratulatory righteousness in dealing with the client.

(4) *Reaching for the moon.* Zeal to see the client be less dependent, value herself more, and command more for herself can make the therapist push too hard and try to move too fast. When these efforts inevitably fail, frustration and anger are in store for the therapist; the client will be left in confusion and despair.

X
YOUR PART IN REFORMATION

*Every woman can do something for
the cause. She who is true to it at her
own fireside, who speaks the right
word to her guests, to her children
and her neighbors' children, does an
educational work as valuable as that
of the woman who speaks from the
platform.*

— *Susan B. Anthony,* History of
Woman Suffrage

FAMILY THERAPY does not explicitly intend to be a social movement. This is an ironic turn of events, for family therapy began in
response to social problems and was nurtured by a strong missionary spirit (Walters, 1985). Whether intended or not, its impact on
individual families, family therapists, family physicians, and the
mental health field leads to an impact on our collective social life
that many declared social movements must envy. This influence
serves either to support or to change prevailing structures of belief
and action regarding family life. Those of us who want this influence to be in the direction of changing prevailing structures must
work to reform fundamental aspects of our professional field.

In the reformation of an established body of thought and practice, people differ in their desire and ability to be visible because
the real or perceived consequences of being visible vary. All types
of activity are welcome. We need in-house spies, undercover
agents, and wolves in sheep's clothing in addition to wild-eyed
radicals who by their mere existence give an otherwise despised
and frightening Middle a more positive connotation.

Below is a (partial) list of actions to further the reformation of family therapy. Some are aimed at sharpening your own awareness. Others are aimed at spreading the word. However you choose to contribute, make sure that if you were ever accused of being a feminist family therapist, there would be enough evidence to convict you.

(1) Since language shapes reality, listen to yourself and your colleagues with a special ear. Usual forms of speech support a sexist outlook, for example: "I'm seeing a man and his wife at 3:30." Suggest alternative phrasing. When the response is "Oh, it doesn't make any difference," note that the impatient reply contradicts itself.

(2) What types of men and women are you most comfortable with as clients? What types of men and women are you least comfortable with as clients? Ask someone to help you assess what your answers indicate about your own journey towards liberation.

(3) At workshops and case conferences, raise questions that force a focus on pertinent feminist issues.

(4) Create new metaphors for power, support, and friendship.

(5) Rent the old movie *Gaslight*. Watch it over and over until you are confident of the meaning of the verb "to gaslight," particularly in this tense: I am being gaslighted. Watch for real-life applications, especially from professors, supervisors, and theorists who are in positions of authority over you.

(6) Gather a group of therapists who will meet weekly with you specifically to address presented cases with a feminist perspective.

(7) Replay some of your favorite old training tapes and view them with a feminist eye. What's new?

(8) Gramsci writes: "One can construct, on a specific practice, a

theory, which, by coinciding and identifying itself with the decisive elements of the practice itself, can accelerate the historical process that is going on, rendering practice more homogeneous, more coherent, more efficient in all its elements, and thus, in other words, developing its potential to the maximum" (1971, p. 365). If people observed your practice, would they know your theory is feminist?

(9) Read Jean Baker Miller's *Toward a New Psychology of Women* (1976). Think about what needs to be written next.

(10) Monitor family therapy journals for sexist language, sexist assumptions, omission of the feminist perspective, silence on gender issues relevant to the discussion. Write the journal and the authors about your observations.

(11) As you evaluate your work, ask yourself: What would be a sexist way to understand this family? What would be a feminist way? What would be a sexist intervention? What would be a feminist intervention?

(12) Subscribe to *Ms.* magazine. Note the parts you especially do not like. Wonder about that. Subscribe to *Cosmopolitan*. Note the parts you especially like. Wonder about that.

(13) When thinking about a family or discussing a family, switch the sex of the identified patient or customer or other key player. What difference does that make in your assessment or treatment plan? Can you defend that difference on feminist grounds?

(14) Rachel Hare-Mustin said, " . . . if we disregard the condition of women, our family therapy may be not worth doing. And, I submit, therapy that is not worth doing, is not worth doing well" (1985). If you were to read those words to your supervisor, would your supervisor agree? If not, what would be your most persuasive reply? Can you get in touch with your supervisor tomorrow? This afternoon?

(15) Read *Portnoy's Complaint* as if you were a feminist family therapist. What changes?

(16) The next time a colleague, student, or client uses the term "girl" to describe a female apparently over the age of sixteen, respond by asking the exact age of the child in question.

(17) Write to AAMFT expressing your disappointment that the study of gender issues is not yet an integral part of the educational requirements for clinical membership.

(18) Read widely. Family therapy is still years behind other social science disciplines in bringing feminism to bear on clinical issues.

(19) If you are involved in the training of future therapists, review your teaching materials to assess how adequately you address the issue of gender, keeping in mind the criterion that it ought to be covered in at least as much depth as generation.

(20) Do a review of your stuck or failed cases over the past few years. Consider how inattention to gender issues might have led to the trouble.

(21) In her poem "To Be of Use," Marge Piercy cautions: "If what we change does not change us/we are playing with blocks" (1973, p. 17). What has changed around your house since you became a feminist?

(22) Consider your initial assessment procedures. Do you inquire about gender roles, tasks, and issues? If not, when will you start?

(23) Listen to the metaphors you, your colleagues, and your clients use. What is really being said about men and women?

(24) Make it your business to find out about the feminism of people running for office in AAMFT and other professional

associations of family therapists. Publicize their responses to you. All other things being equal, vote for women candidates.

(25) Take a sexist to lunch. Ask for a recounting of an interesting case currently in treatment. Raise questions that confound and enlighten.

(26) When you read an article or book that is especially good at shaking the foundations, circulate it among your colleagues and teachers — anonymously, if necessary.

(27) Virginia Goldner writes: " . . . as we struggle with the clinical particulars of each family case, we ought to at least be aware of how we participate in, and what it would mean to challenge, the structures of thought and the structuring of power that keep women (and therefore their families) trapped in cycles of toxic devotion and recrimination" (1985, p. 44). Feel into the phrase "toxic devotion." Apply it to yourself and to your women clients. What does that make you want to do?

(28) Does your file on resources for clients include shelters for battered women, a feminist gynecologist, a feminist lawyer, the women's studies coordinator at the nearest university, the local rape crisis hotline, the nearest women's support group?

(29) Read Adrienne Rich's "Compulsory Heterosexuality and Lesbian Existence" (1980). Think about what officials would do with that article if they knew about it.

(30) William J. Goode writes: "We must never underestimate the cunning or the staying power of those in charge" (1982, p. 133). What are you doing to maintain your energy so that you can outsmart and outlast them?

REFERENCES

Abbott, S., & Love, B. (1977). *Sappho was a right-on woman: A liberated view of lesbianism*. New York: Stein and Day.

Alther, L. (1984). *Other women*. New York: Knopf.

Anthony, S. B. (1902). *History of woman suffrage*. As quoted by McPhee, C., & Fitzgerald, A. (1979). *Feminist quotations: Voices of rebels, reformers and visionaries*. New York: Crowell.

Aries, P. (1962). *Centuries of childhood: A social history of family life* (R. Baldick, Trans.). London: Cape. (Original work published 1960)

Atwood, M. (1986). *The handmaid's tale*. Boston: Houghton Mifflin.

Avis, J. M. (1985). The politics of functional family therapy: A feminist critique. *Journal of Marital and Family Therapy, 11*(2), 127–138.

Avis, J. M. (in press). Deepening awareness: A private study guide to feminism and family therapy. *Journal of Psychotherapy and the Family*.

Baetz, R. (1980). *Lesbian crossroads: Personal stories of lesbian struggles and triumphs*. New York: Morrow.

Barnett, J. (1971). Narcissism and dependency in the obsessional-hysteric marriage. *Family Process, 10*, 75–84.

Bartolome, F. (1972). Executives as human beings. *Harvard Business Review, 50*, 62–69.

de Beauvoir, S. (1974). *The second sex*. New York: Vintage/Random House.

Bergman, I. (1987). Creative and powerful ways of working with families. Workshop presented at the University of Houston-Clear Lake.

Bernard, J. (1971). *Women and the public interest*. New York: Aldine Atherton.

Bernard, J. (1972). *The future of marriage*. New Haven: Yale University Press.

Bernard, J. (1982). *The future of marriage* (2nd ed.). New Haven: Yale University Press.

Bernikow, L. (1980). *Among women*. New York: Harper Colophon.

Bograd, M. (1984). Family systems approaches to wife-battering: A feminist critique. *American Journal of Orthopsychiatry, 54*, 558–563.

Bowen, M. (1966). The use of family theory in clinical practice. *Comprehensive Psychiatry, 7*(5), 345–374.

Brandwein, R. A., Brown, C. A., & Fox, E. M. (1974). Women and children last: The social situation of divorced mothers and their families. *Journal of Marriage and the Family, 36*, 498–514.

Broverman, I., Vogel, S. R., Broverman, D. M., Clarkson, F. E., & Rosenkrantz, P. S. (1972). Sex role stereotypes: A current appraisal. *Journal of Social Issues, 28*, 59–78.

Brown, R. M. (1976). *Autobiography of my mother*. Garden City, NY: Doubleday.

Brownmiller, S. (1984). *Femininity*. New York: Simon & Schuster.

Caplan, P. J. (1985). *The myth of women's masochism*. New York: Dutton.

Caplan, P. J., & Hall-McCorquodale, I. (1985). Mother-blaming in major clinical journals. *American Journal of Orthopsychiatry, 55*, 345–353.

Carter, E. (1986). Success in family therapy. *The Family Therapy Networker, 10*(4), 17–22.

Carter, E., Papp, P., Silverstein, O., & Walters, M. (1984a). *Mothers and daughters* (Monograph Series Vol. 1, No. 1). Washington, DC: The Women's Project in Family Therapy.

Carter, E., Papp, P., Silverstein, O., & Walters, M. (1984b). *Mothers and sons, fathers and daughters* (Monograph Series Vol. 2, No. 1). Washington, DC: The Women's Project in Family Therapy.

Cashion, B. G. (1982). Female-headed families: Effects on children and clinical implications. *Journal of Marital and Family Therapy, 8*(2), 77–86.

Caust, B., Libow, J., & Raskin, P. (1981). Challenges and promises of training women as family systems therapists. *Family Process, 20*(4), 439–447.

Chernin, K. (1981). *The obsession: Reflections on the tyranny of slenderness*. New York: Harper and Row.

Chernin, K. (1983). *In my mother's house: A daughter's story*. New York: Harper Colophon.

Chesler, P. (1972). *Women and madness*. Garden City, NY: Doubleday.

Chodorow, N. (1978). *The reproduction of mothering: Psychoanalysis and the sociology of gender*. Berkeley: University of California Press.

Clark, R. A., Nye, F. I., & Gecas, V. (1978). Husband's work involvement and marital role performance. *Journal of Marriage and the Family, 40*, 9–21.

Conklin, G. H. (1981). Cultural determinants of power for women in the family: A neglected aspect of family research. In G. Kurian, & R. Ghosh (Eds.), *Women in the family and the economy* (pp. 9–27). Westport, CT: Greenwood.

Daly, M. (1973). *Beyond God the Father: Toward a philosophy of women's liberation*. Boston: Beacon.

Daly, M. (1978). *Gyn/Ecology*. Boston: Beacon.

Davis, A. Y. (1981). *Women, race, and class*. New York: Random House.

Deutsch, H. (1944). *The psychology of women*. New York: Grune & Stratton.

Dinnerstein, D. (1977). *The mermaid and the minotaur: Sexual arrangements and human malaise*. New York: Harper & Row.

REFERENCES

Dobash, R., & Dobash, R. (1979). *Violence against wives*. New York: Free Press.

Ehrenreich, B. (1983). *The hearts of men*. Garden City, NY: Anchor.

Ehrenreich, B., & English, D. (1978). *For her own good: 150 years of advice to women*. New York: Doubleday/Anchor.

Elshtain, J. B. (1982). Feminist discourse and its discontents: Language, power, and meaning. In N. O. Keohane, M. Z. Rosaldo, & B. C. Gelpi (Eds.). *Feminist theory: A critique of ideology* (pp. 143–144). Chicago: The University of Chicago Press.

French, M. (1985). *Beyond power: On women, men, and morals*. New York: Summit.

Freud, S. (1959). The economic problem in masochism. In E. Jones (Ed.) & J. Riviere (Trans.), Sigmund Freud: Collected papers (Vol. 2, pp. 255–268). New York: Basic Books. (Original work published 1924)

Friedan, B. (1963). *The feminine mystique*. New York: Norton.

Friedman, M., & Rosenman, R. (1981). *Type A behavior and your heart*. New York: Fawcett.

Fulmer, R. H. (1983). A structural approach to unresolved mourning in single parent family systems. *Journal of Marital and Family Therapy, 9*(3), 259–269.

Gartrell, N. (1984). Issues in psychotherapy with lesbian women. *Work in Progress*. (Available from Stone Center for Developmental Services and Studies, Wellesley, MA)

Genovese, E. (1974). *Roll, Jordan, roll: The world the slaves made*. New York: Pantheon.

Gilligan, C. (1982). *In a different voice: Psychological theory and woman's development*. Cambridge: Harvard University Press.

Gilman, C. P. (1973a). Women and economics. In A. S. Rossi (Ed.), *The feminist papers* (pp. 572–598). New York: Bantam. (Original work published 1898)

Gilman, C. P. (1973b). *The yellow wallpaper*. New York: Feminist Press. (Original work published 1899)

Glennon, L. M. (1983). Synthesism: A case of feminist methodology. In G. Morgan (Ed.), *Beyond method: Strategies for social research* (pp. 260–271). Beverly Hills: Sage.

Glick, P. C. (1979). Future American families. *Cofo Memo II, 3*, 1–3.

Goldner, V. (1985a). Feminism and family therapy. *Family Process, 24*(1), 31–47.

Goldner, V. (1985b). Warning: Family therapy may be dangerous to your health. *The Family Therapy Networker, 9*(6), 19–23.

Goode, W. J. (1982). Why men resist. In B. Thorne (Ed.), *Rethinking the family: Some feminist questions* (pp. 131–150). New York: Longman.

Goodman, B. (1980). *"Where will you be?" The professional oppression of gay people: A lesbian feminist perspective*. West Hempstead, NY: Womenmade Products.

Gramsci, A. (1971). *Selections from the prison notebooks*. New York: International.

Gould, L. (1976). *A sea change*. New York: Avon.

Griffin, S. (1978). *Woman and nature: The roaring inside her*. New York: Harper Colophon.

Griffith, E. (1984). *In her own right: The life of Elizabeth Cady Stanton*. New York: Oxford University Press.

Gulotta, T. P. (1981). The corporate family: Theory and treatment. *Journal of Marital and Family Therapy, 7*(2), 151–158.

Hacker, A. (1982, March 18). Farewell to the family? *New York Review of Books*, pp. 17–20.

Haley, J. (1971). Toward a theory of pathological systems. In G. H. Zuk & I. Boszormenyi-Nagy (Eds.), *Family therapy and disturbed families* (pp. 11–27). Palo Alto: Science and Behavior Books.

Hare-Mustin, R. (1978). A feminist approach to family therapy. *Family Process, 17*, 181–194.

Hare-Mustin, R. (1985). *Family therapy of the future: A feminist critique.* Paper presented at the meeting of the American Association for Marriage and Family Therapy, New York.

Hare-Mustin, R. (1987). The problem of gender in family therapy theory. *Family Process, 26*(1), 15–28.

Herman, J. (1982). *Father-daughter incest.* Cambridge: Harvard University Press.

Hidalgo, H., Peterson, T. L., & Woodman, N. J. (Eds.). (1985). *Lesbian and gay issues: A resource manual for social workers.* Silver Spring, MD: National Association of Social Workers.

Hines, P. M., & Boyd-Franklin, N. (1982). Black families. In M. McGoldrick, J. Pearce, & J. Giordano (Eds.), *Ethnicity and family therapy* (pp. 84–107). New York: Guilford.

Hoffmann, L. (1981). *Foundations of family therapy: A conceptual framework for systems change.* New York: Basic Books.

Ibsen, H. J. (1985). A doll's house. In M. Meyer (Ed. and Trans.), *The plays of Ibsen, Vol. I.* New York: Washington Square Press. (Original work published 1879)

James, K., & McIntyre, D. (1983). The reproduction of families: The social role of family? *Journal of Marital and Family Therapy, 9*(2), 119–129.

Kanter, R. M. (1977). *Men and women of the corporation.* New York: Basic.

Kerr, M. E. (1981). Family systems theory and therapy. In A. S. Gurman & D. P. Kniskern (Eds.), *Handbook of family therapy* (pp. 226–266). New York: Brunner/Mazel.

Kosof, A. (1985). *Incest.* New York: Watts.

Kramer, J. (1985). *Family interfaces: Transgenerational patterns.* New York: Brunner/Mazel.

Krauskopf, J. (1977). Partnership marriage. In J. Chapman & M. Gates (Eds.), *Women into wives* (pp. 93–121). Beverly Hills: Sage.

Krestan, J. & Bepko, C. (1980). The problem of fusion in the lesbian relationship. *Family Process, 19*(3), 277–290.

Lerner, G. (1986). *The creation of patriarchy.* New York: Oxford.

Lewis, S. (1979). *Sunday's women: Lesbian life today.* Boston: Beacon.

Libow, J. A., Raskin, P. A., & Caust, B. L. (1982). Feminist and family systems therapy: Are they irreconcilable? *The American Journal of Family Therapy, 10*, 3–12.

Loulan, J. A. (1984). *Lesbian sex.* San Francisco: Spinsters Ink.

Maccoby, M. (1976). The corporate climber has to find his heart. *Fortune, 94*, 98–108.

McCrindle, J., & Rowbotham, S. (1983). *Dutiful daughters.* Middlesex, England: Penguin.

MacKinnon, C. A. (1987). *Feminism unmodified: Discourses on life and law.* Cambridge: Harvard University Press.

Margolin, G., Fernandez, R., Talovic, S., & Onorato, R. (1983). Sex role considerations and behavioral marital therapy: Equal does not mean identical. *Journal of Marital and Family Therapy, 9*(2), 131–145.

Masnick, G., & Bane, M. J. (1980). *The nation's families: 1960–1990*. Boston: Auburn House.

Mead, M. (1949). *Male and female: A study of the sexes in a changing world*. New York: Morrow.

Miller, A. (1981). *The drama of the gifted child*. New York: Basic.

Miller, J. B. (1976). *Toward A New Psychology of Women*. Boston: Beacon.

Miller, J. B. (1982). Women and power. *Work in Progress*. (Available from Stone Center for Developmental Services and Studies, Wellesley, MA.)

Mills, C. W. (1951). *White collar: The American middle classes*. New York: Oxford University Press.

Mintz, S., & Kellogg, S. (1987). *Domestic revolutions: A social history of American family life*. New York: Free Press.

Minuchin, S. (1974). *Families and family therapy*. Cambridge: Harvard University Press.

Morawetz, A., & Walker, G. (1984). *Brief therapy with single-parent families*. New York: Brunner/Mazel.

Morgan, E. W. (1966). *The Puritan family*. New York: Harper & Row.

Morgan, R. (1968). *Going too far: The personal chronicle of a feminist*. New York: Random House.

Moynihan, D. P. (1971). The Negro family: The case for national action. In J. H. Bracey, A. Meier, & E. Rudwick (Eds.), *Black matriarch: Myth or reality* (pp. 126–159). Belmont, CA: Wadsworth. (Original work published 1965)

Napier, A. Y., with Whitaker, C. A. (1978). *The family crucible*. New York: Harper and Row.

Norgren, J. (1982). In search of a national child-care policy: Background and prospects. In E. Boneparth (Ed.), *Women, power, and policy* (pp. 124–143). New York: Pergamon.

Norwood, R. (1985). *Women who love too much*. New York: Simon and Schuster.

Oakley, A. (1974). *Woman's work: The housewife, past and present*. New York: Pantheon.

Orbach, S. (1978). *Fat is a feminist issue*. New York: Paddington Press.

Papp, P. (1984). Foreword. In A. Morawetz, & G. Walker, *Brief therapy with single-parent families* (pp. vii–ix). New York: Brunner/Mazel.

Philipson, I. (1985). Gender and narcissism. *Psychology of Women Quarterly, 9*, 213–228.

Piercy, M. (1973). A shadow play for guilt. *To be of use*. Garden City, New York: Doubleday.

Pittman, F. (1985). Gender myths. *The Family Therapy Networker, 9*(6), 24–32.

Pogrebin, L. C. (1983). *Family politics*. New York: McGraw-Hill.

Porter, C. (1948). So in love. Minneapolis: Hal Leonard.

Rabb, T. K., & Rotberg, R. I. (Eds.). (1973). *The family in history*. New York: Harper & Row.

Rich, A. (1976). *Of woman born: Motherhood as experience and institution*. New York: Norton.

Rich, A. (1978). *The dream of a common language: Poems 1974–1977*. New York: Norton.

Rich, A. (1979). *On lies, secrets, and silence: Selected prose 1966–1978*. New York: Norton.

Rich, A. (1980). Compulsory heterosexuality and lesbian existence. *Signs, 5*(4), 631–660.

Rich, A. (1986). *Blood, bread, and poetry: Selected prose 1979–1985*. New York: Norton.

Roazen, P. (1985). *Helene Deutsch: A psychoanalyst's life*. New York: Anchor.

Roth, S. (1985). Psychotherapy with lesbian couples: Individual issues, female socialization, and the social context. *Journal of Marital and Family Therapy, 11*(3), 273–286.

Russell, D. (1982). *Rape in marriage*. New York: Macmillan.

Safire, W. (1987, May 10). The modifiers of mother. *The New York Times Magazine*, pp. 10–12.

Satchell, M. (1987, April 29). Could you, er, say that again? *U. S. News and World Report*, p. 71.

Schecter, S. (1982). *Women and male violence*. Boston: South End Press.

Seidenberg, R. (1973). *Corporate wives — corporate casualties?* New York: AMACOM.

Shainess, N. (1984). *Sweet suffering: Woman as victim*. Indianapolis: Bobbs-Merrill.

Simon, R. (Ed.). (1985). Feminism: Shedding new light on the family. *The Family Therapy Networker* (Special Issue), *9*(6).

Skolnick, A. S. (1983). *The intimate environment: Exploring marriage and the family*. Boston: Little, Brown.

Skynner, A. C. R. (1976). *Systems of family and marital psychotherapy*. New York: Brunner/Mazel.

Stiver, I. P. (1984). The meaning of "dependency" in female-male relationships. *Work in Progress*. (Available from Stone Center for Developmental Services and Studies, Wellesley, MA)

Stolorow, R. D. (1975). The narcissistic function of masochism and sadism. *International Journal of Psychoanalysis, 56*, 441–447.

Straus, M., Gelles, R., & Steinmetz, S. (1980). *Behind closed doors: Violence in the American family*. Garden City, New York: Anchor.

Swerdow, A. (Ed.). (1978). *Feminist perspectives on housework and child care*. Bronxville, New York: Sarah Lawrence College.

Taggart, M. (1985). The feminist critique in epistemological perspective: Questions of context in family therapy. *Journal of Marital and Family Therapy, 11*(2), 113–126.

Thorne, B. (Ed.). (1982). *Rethinking the family: Some feminist questions*. New York: Longman.

Tilly, L., & Scott, J. (1978). *Women, work, and family*. New York: Holt, Rinehart, & Winston.

de Tocqueville, A. (1986). *Democracy in America* (F. Bowen, Trans.). Darby, PA: Arden Library. (Original work published 1835)

United States Census. (1978). *Current population reports*. Washington, DC: U.S. Government Printing Office.

United States Department of Commerce National Data Book and Guide to Sources. (1987). *Statistical abstract of the United States*. Washington, DC: U.S. Government Printing Office.

Vida, G. (Ed.). (1978). *Our right to love*. Englewood Cliffs, NJ: Prentice-Hall.

Walker, A. (1982). *The color purple*. New York: Harcourt Brace Jovanovich.

Walker, A. (1983). *In search of our mother's gardens: Womanist prose*. New York: Harcourt Brace Jovanovich.

Walker, L. E. (1979). *The battered woman*. New York: Harper & Row.

Walters, M. (1984). Fathers and daughters. In E. Carter, P. Papp, O. Silverstein, & M. Walters, *Mothers and sons, fathers and daughters*. (Monograph Series Vol. 2, No. 1). Washington, DC: The Women's Project in Family Therapy.

Walters, M. (1985). Where have all the flowers gone? *The Family Therapy Networker, 9*(4), 38–41.

Watzlawick, P., Weakland, J., & Fisch, R. (1974). *Change: Principles of problem formation and problem resolution*. New York: Norton.

Weiss, R. S. (1979). Growing up a little faster: The experience of growing up in a single-parent household. *Journal of Social Issues, 35*, 97–111.

Wheeler, D., Avis, J. M., Miller, L., & Chaney, S. (1985). Rethinking family therapy education and supervision: A feminist model. *Journal of Psychotherapy and the Family, 1*, 53–71.

Woolf, V. (1929). *A room of one's own*. New York: Harcourt Brace Jovanovich.

INDEX